Plated

by Parth

ADVANCE PRAISE FOR THE BOOK

'Parth Bajaj is a true artist in the world of baking. His passion, creativity and dedication are evident in every creation he shares, whether on screen or on social media. What makes Parth stand out is not just his talent but also his generous spirit—he is always ready to teach, inspire and make baking accessible to all. This book is a beautiful reflection of that spirit. It's more than just a collection of recipes; it's a guiding hand for children and young bakers stepping into the magical world of baking. Parth's clear instructions, playful energy and top-notch techniques will undoubtedly ignite confidence and joy in every reader. I wholeheartedly recommend this book to anyone who wants to bake with love, learn with ease and dream big—just like Parth does'—**Chef Ajay Chopra**

'From the very start, Parth's passion for baking has been matched only by his desire to lift others up. Through workshops, online recipes, heartfelt conversations and now this book, he's become a guide to so many on their baking journey. This is more than a collection of recipes—it's a generous offering from someone who truly believes that baking can bring people together, inspire creativity and change lives'—**Chef Pooja Dhingra**

'A young chef's first book is more than just recipes—it's a journey of passion, creativity and bold flavours. Each page tells a story, each dish a reflection of his evolving artistry. #shineon' —**Chef Vicky Ratnani**

'*Plated by Parth* is more than just a recipe book. It's thoughtful, delicious and a true gift for every aspiring baker'—**Chef Sanjyot Keer**

Plated

by Parth

Whisk, Bake,
Indulge

PARTH BAJAJ

EBURY
PRESS

An imprint of Penguin Random House

EBURY PRESS

Ebury Press is an imprint of the Penguin Random House group of companies
whose addresses can be found at global.penguinrandomhouse.com

Published by Penguin Random House India Pvt. Ltd
4th Floor, Capital Tower 1, MG Road,
Gurugram 122 002, Haryana, India

First published in Ebury Press by Penguin Random House India 2025

ISBN 9780143470151

Book design by Neeraj Nath
Typeset in Adobe Caslon Pro by Manipal Technologies Limited, Manipal
Printed at Replika Press Pvt. Ltd, India

www.penguin.co.in

Foreword

It's often said that the true joy of baking lies in the journey of experimenting, learning and creating something beautiful with your hands. When you have had the privilege of working in the kitchen for as long as I have, you realize that baking is not just about following recipes. It's about understanding the chemistry of ingredients, having the patience to perfect each step and, most importantly, putting love into every creation.

That is exactly what *Plated by Parth* represents. With this book, Parth takes a step further in his mission to make baking a joyful and accessible experience for all. It's more than just a collection of recipes; it's a celebration of the art of baking. Whether you are baking for a special occasion or simply indulging yourself, every dessert in these pages is meant to bring happiness to those who experience it. Parth's recipes will not only help you create delicious treats but also make the process of baking truly enjoyable.

What makes this book stand out is not just the impressive range of recipes it offers but also the heart and soul Parth has poured into each one of them. From rich and indulgent eggless brownies to vegan cakes, and from classic layered desserts

to no-bake treats, there truly is something for everyone. Whether you are a beginner or a seasoned baker, Parth's approach to simplifying baking techniques will give you the confidence to create masterpieces in your own kitchen.

Parth has an exceptional ability to blend technical precision with creativity. His attention to detail and dedication to sharing his knowledge make this book more than just a collection of recipes. I invite you all to dive into this book with an open heart and a hungry stomach. *Plated by Parth* is more than just a cookbook; it is a testament to the joy of baking, and I am certain it will inspire you to create your own sweet moments.

It fills me with pride to see a young talent like him carving his niche in the world of baking. With this book, he takes a step forward in his mission to make baking an enjoyable and accessible experience for all. I wholeheartedly wish him great success and offer my heartfelt blessings for this endeavour. His journey is only just beginning, and I cannot wait to see where it takes him.

CHEF SANJEEV KAPOOR

Some General Tips and Tricks to Ace the Recipes in This Book

- While it might seem obvious to some, it is worth mentioning for the budding bakers out there: Always . . . always accurately measure every ingredient before you start baking for the best results. This is known as *mise en place*, which refers to keeping all the ingredients ready.

- Speaking of measuring, I highly recommend measuring everything by weight instead of by volume. A kitchen scale barely costs anything and should last you years. Most of the recipes in this book have measurements both in grams and in cups, but if possible, try to measure by weight. It's far more accurate that way.

- For almost all recipes, always preheat your oven 15–20 mins prior to baking. This ensures you get a consistent heat source throughout the baking time. If you wish to, you can invest in an oven thermometer, again a super affordable tool to have.

- Whenever you're making any kind of batters or cookie/pie doughs that involve gluten, avoid over-mixing them, otherwise the end result will be dense. Unless, of course, you're working with bread doughs; that's where you want the gluten to develop.

- Whenever you're working with cake tins, it's always best to start by greasing them with oil or butter. Then line them with parchment paper and finally dust them with some flour. This ensures a smooth release from the tin.

- Always let the baked goods cool down in their tins/trays before disturbing them or de-moulding them. Impatience can ruin a perfectly baked treat.

- This one also might sound very obvious, but please use best-quality ingredients for best possible results. Especially while working with chocolate or fruits.

- When you're baking a dish for the first time, it's a good rule of thumb to follow everything in the recipe to a T. Then you can start playing around with variations.

- Always sift your dry ingredients, no matter what you're making. This has multiple reasons and benefits. First, you get rid of lumps. Second, you get rid of impurities, if any. And third, the batter gets aerated, resulting in a softer and lighter crumb.

- For various applications, you'd need your ingredients to be at different temperatures and textures, so read the requirements and prepare everything accordingly. This plays a huge role in deciding the texture and consistency of the final dish.

- That being said, if the recipe doesn't specify a particular temperature, always use room-temperature ingredients, with some exceptions, such as whipping cream, ice, frostings, etc.

- Sometimes recipes call for various egg sizes, so pay attention to that and choose the eggs accordingly. If it's not specified, feel free to use medium ones.

- Whenever you're adding any add-ons to a batter, say, chocolate chips or berries, always coat them with some flour. This helps to avoid the sinking of those add-ons to the bottom of the cake tin.

- Use good-quality vanilla extract, if not a proper vanilla pod. Ditch the commercial low-quality vanilla essence. That's not real vanilla. The best way to tell if you're using the good stuff is to just look at the label—if it reads 'extract', then it's the real product. But if it's 'essence' or 'flavour', then it's not. Vanilla extract is also thicker in consistency and has small specks in it.

- *Always* add a pinch of salt to all desserts. This is something I swear by and highly recommend in order to bring out an even better flavour of any dessert. Salt not only balances the sweetness, it also enhances the flavour of the other ingredients.

- Check the expiry dates of your baking powder, baking soda and yeast (leavening agents basically). You don't want to end up with flat cakes and dense breads after putting in all the hard work. So, make sure you keep an eye on it.

- You must have heard the phrase 'Bake it until a skewer inserted comes out clean.' Although that's mostly true, it can sometimes be misleading or a bit tricky to follow. So, I personally prefer poking the cakes lightly with my finger; if they spring back up, it means they're done baking.

- Talking about baking, I always let stuff like brownies, cheesecakes, puddings and other delicate desserts cool off for 3–5 mins in the turned-off oven before taking them out. This provides them with a buffer environment, which in turn reduces the temperature gradually and not instantly. This helps to avoid the sinking of those desserts.

- As a rule of thumb, it's a great idea to always chill your cookie dough. This helps with multiple things: firstly, the dough becomes easier to handle. Secondly, the gluten gets time to relax. Thirdly, it controls the spread of your cookies and lastly, the cookies turn out chewier this way.

- If you can't find unsalted butter, you can use salted butter too, but make sure you skip the additional salt mentioned in most recipes.

General Egg Substitutions

Although eggs make baking so much simpler, we sometimes need to convert an egg-based recipe into an egg-free one since many folks don't consume them—be it for religious reasons, dietary reasons or allergy issues. This simple and easy-to-follow substitution chart will help you bake some of your favourite desserts without eggs, if not all of them.

Please note: These are general suggestions and may not work well with some recipes. Some recipes can only be made with eggs, while others may require a lot of other tweaks and merely substituting an ingredient won't be enough.

As a general rule of thumb, 1 medium whole egg = ¼ cup in volume. So whichever substitute you're going for has to be ¼ cup as well (generally).

For Cakes and Cupcakes

1 egg = ¼ cup mashed banana (around half a banana)
1 egg = ¼ cup yogurt/curd
1 egg = ¼ cup apple sauce

For Cookies

1 egg = 1 flax egg* (1 tbsp flax seed powder + 3 tbsp water)
1 egg = 3 tbsp milk
1 egg = ¼ cup sweetened condensed milk

For Brownies

1 egg = 1 flax egg (1 tbsp flax seed powder + 3 tbsp water)
1 egg = ¼ cup apple sauce
1 egg = ¼ cup aquafaba (chickpea water)

For Meringue-Based Desserts

1 egg = ¼ cup aquafaba (chickpea water)

For Egg Wash

1 egg = 1 tbsp whole milk + 1 tbsp cream + 2 tsp honey + a pinch of salt

For Custards

1 egg = 2 tbsp cornflour + 3 tbsp milk

For Breads

1 egg = 1 tbsp ground chia seeds + ⅓ cup water (This is similar to flax egg but made with chia seeds. This works well as a binder for breads that require eggs as a binding agent.)

For Desserts Where Eggs Are the Leavening Agents

1 egg = 1 tbsp vinegar + 1 tsp baking soda

Flax egg is a popular egg substitute that is made by mixing ground flax seeds with water. All you have to do is just mix them and let them sit for 5 mins, after which, the consistency of the mixture should resemble eggs. It works beautifully well. But my favourite egg substitute for cookies has to be whole milk.

CONTENTS

BARS AND BROWNIES

CARAMELIZED WALNUT BLONDIES

'Because not all brownies need to have dark chocolate to taste bomb.'

INGREDIENTS

½ cup (115 g) melted butter
1 cup (100 g) brown sugar
1 egg
½ tsp vanilla extract
A few drops almond extract (optional)
A pinch of salt
1 cup (120 g) all-purpose flour
⅓ cup white chocolate chips
¼ cup (30 g) chopped walnuts

STEPS

1. Preheat the oven to 170 °C.
2. Whisk together melted butter and brown sugar until they're completely mixed, then add in your egg, vanilla extract and almond extract, which is totally optional. Give it a whisk.
3. Sift in your all-purpose flour and salt. Cut and fold the batter until it's just combined.
4. Then it's time to add in your white chocolate chips and chopped walnuts. Fold everything until it's all just barely mixed, don't over mix.
5. Transfer the batter to a 7-inch square lined baking tin, spread it out evenly and top with some extra white chocolate chips and walnuts.
6. Bake in a preheated oven at 170 °C for 25 mins.
7. Let it cool completely and then cut it into nine bars and serve fresh :)

Pro Tips

1. Always use good-quality ingredients.
2. Don't over mix the batter at any stage, as that might lead to excess gluten formation.

Serves: 9   **Prep time:** *10 mins*   **Bake time:** *25 mins*

BLUEBERRY CHEESECAKE BARS

'When I made this for the first time, the entire batch got over within a few minutes without us even realizing.'

INGREDIENTS

1 cup crushed biscuits or
120 g digestive biscuits
¼ cup (60 g) melted
butter
1⅓ cup (337 g) cream
cheese
2 tbsp (30 g) all-purpose
flour
1 cup (112 g) icing sugar
⅔ cup (150 g) fresh cream
1 tsp vanilla extract
Zest of ½ a lemon
1 cup (150 g) frozen or
fresh blueberries

STEPS

1. Preheat your oven to 150 °C.
2. Line a 7-inch square cake tin and cover the sides with parchment paper. Grind all of your biscuits and melt your butter. Mix both of them nicely to form a wet sand consistency. Form a crust for the cheesecake using a measuring cup or a spoon. Refrigerate the crust for 15–20 mins at least.
3. Add your cream cheese and icing sugar to a bowl. Mix both of them well, add in your fresh cream and flour, and mix them as well. Add your vanilla essence and lemon zest.
4. Gently fold in your blueberries (preserve some for placing on top of the batter).
5. Transfer this batter to your prepared crust.
6. Prepare a water bath* and bake in a preheated oven at 150 °C for 40–45 mins.
7. Let it cool completely in the fridge overnight before de-moulding and cutting.

Pro Tips
1. Don't use dried berries for this recipe. Use either fresh or frozen ones.
2. You can make this with any other berry as well 🙂
3. Let the cheesecake cool completely before de-moulding and cutting.

---

* To create a water bath, heat a few cups of water and pour it in a baking tray. Place this baking tray on the lower rack of the oven and then place your cheesecake tin on another baking tray. Place the cheesecake tray on the middle rack of the oven.

Serves: *9*   **Prep time:** *25 mins*   **Bake time:** *45 mins*

NUTELLA FERRERO BROWNIES

'Brownies were the first dessert I baked, so you can imagine how seriously I take them. I baked my first brownie nearly at the age of sixteen. My recipe has evolved so much, yet it feels so nostalgic every single time I bake a brownie, just like eating a spoonful of Nutella. This brownie recipe tastes just like that, a spoonful of nostalgia.'

INGREDIENTS

Approx. 1 cup (150 g) dark chocolate
Approx. ½ cup (100 g) unsalted butter
½ cup (100 g) caster sugar
½ cup (100 g) brown sugar
2 eggs
½ cup + 1 tbsp (75 g) all-purpose flour
1 tbsp (14 g) cocoa powder
1 tsp instant coffee
¼ tsp salt
9–10 Ferrero Rochers
⅔ cup (200 g) Nutella

STEPS

1. Line a 7-inch brownie tin with parchment paper and spread your Nutella in it. Freeze it for a few hours.
2. Preheat your oven to 170 °C.
3. Melt the dark chocolate and butter together using a microwave or a double boiler set-up. Add in your instant coffee while this happens, so that it can 'brew'.
4. In a separate bowl, add both of your sugars along with the eggs.
5. Whisk everything for just about a minute, not too long. You don't want too much air in the batter, otherwise your brownies might sink.
6. Add in your melted chocolate butter mixture and give it a whisk.
7. Time to sift all your dry ingredients: all-purpose flour, cocoa powder and salt.
8. Gently fold the batter until it's just combined.
9. Chop up 4–5 pieces of Ferrero Rochers and add those to your batter.
10. Combine those and transfer half of the batter to a lined 7-inch square tin. Top it off with your frozen Nutella layer followed by your remaining batter.
11. Top the batter with nine Ferrero Rochers halves so that all the brownies have one piece each.
12. Bake at 170 c for 35 mins or until a skewer inserter comes out slightly sticky.
13. Let the brownies settle in the turned off oven for 5 mins and continue to cool them at room temperature for at least an hour.
14. Cut into nine equal pieces with a sharp knife and enjoy!

Pro Tips

1. My secret for the perfect brownies is to refrigerate the brownie batter before baking for 30–40 mins (once it's in the tin).
2. Try leaving the baked brownies inside the turned off oven for 5 mins so that they don't sink at all.

Serves: 9   **Prep time:** *15 mins*   **Bake time:** *35 mins*

ROASTED CASHEW FUDGE

'I have made fudge countless times. For the most amount of time, it was just using almonds, walnuts or hazelnuts. Until I realized that the cashew chocolate roll at Haldiram's is one of the best sweets ever. Chocolate and cashew are such an underrated combination. Well, not any more.'

INGREDIENTS

⅔ cup (100 g) cashews
1 ¾ cup (400 g)
sweetened condensed milk
1 cup (150 g) dark
chocolate, chopped

STEPS

1. Start by roasting your cashews in a non-stick pan until they're slightly coloured and fragrant.
2. Let them cool off, then chop them into uneven-sized pieces.
3. In the same pan, add your condensed milk and dark chocolate.
4. Start cooking them at medium heat while stirring constantly.
5. The chocolate will melt within seconds, but you'll feel like nothing is changing for a while afterwards. But make sure to keep stirring it constantly.
6. After a few minutes, the mixture will start to thicken.
7. Keep cooking until the fudge starts to leave the pan.
8. At that moment, add in most of your chopped cashews and quickly fold them in.
9. Transfer the fudge to a lined 7-inch square cake tin.
10. Top it off with the remaining chopped cashews.
11. Cover and let it set for 6–8 hours or overnight at room temperature.
12. Cut into desired pieces using a sharp knife.
13. This is super addictive so try it at your own risk :)

Pro Tips
1. Make sure to constantly stir the fudge mixture otherwise the chocolate may burn.
2. You can use any other nuts in place of cashews.

Serves: *9*   **Prep time:** *15 mins*

MILLIONAIRE SHORTBREAD BARS

'This dish forced my non-foodie friend to ask for a recipe for the first time.'

INGREDIENTS

Shortbread Base

1 ½ cup (175 g) all-purpose flour
⅓ cup (40 g) icing sugar
½ cup (100 g) cold butter
1 tsp cold milk or 1 small egg yolk

Caramel

1 ¾ cup (400 g) condensed milk
½ cup (100 g) unsalted butter
3 tbsp (40 g) sugar
½ tsp salt

Chocolate

1 ¼ cup (200 g) dark chocolate
3 tbsp + 1 tsp (50 g) cream

STEPS

1. Start by combining flour and icing sugar in a mixing bowl.
2. Add in the cold chopped butter and blend it in the dry ingredients with the help of a pastry blender or a whisk or a fork. You could also use a food processor for this.
3. Bind the dough by adding a splash of cold milk or an egg yolk if you eat those.
4. Press the dough evenly in an 8-inch lined square tin. Prick holes in it using a fork.
5. Bake in a preheated oven at 180 °C for 16–18 mins or until its lightly coloured.
6. Meanwhile, add condensed milk, butter, sugar and salt to a saucepan.
7. Cook on medium heat while whisking it constantly until the mixture thickens.
8. Continue to cook until the caramel turns bubbly and light golden in colour.
9. Pour it over your prepared crust and bake once again for 5–6 mins.
10. Prepare a ganache by melting chocolate and cream together in a double boiler.
11. Let the dish come to room temperature and then pour the melted chocolate mixture over it, refrigerate overnight or at least for 4 hours.
12. Cut into nine equal pieces using a sharp knife and devour!

Pro Tip

1. If the dough feels dry or difficult to bind, you can add a splash of milk to the shortbread dough.

Serves: *9*   **Prep time:** *20 mins*   **Bake time:** *25 mins*

ULTIMATE BISCOFF BROWNIES

'If I had to bake only one brownie for the rest of my life, it'd be this one—it's that good.'

INGREDIENTS

1 cup (150 g) dark chocolate
½ cup (100 g) unsalted butter
½ cup (100 g) caster sugar
½ cup (100 g) brown sugar
2 eggs
½ cup + 1 tbsp (75 g) all-purpose flour
1 tbsp (14 g) cocoa powder
A dash of vanilla
¼ tsp salt
½ cup (100 g) biscoff spread
10–12 biscoff biscuits

STEPS

1. Preheat the oven to 170 °C.
2. Add your Biscoff spread to a piping bag or just use a spoon for this recipe.
3. Melt your dark chocolate and butter together using a microwave or a double boiler set-up.
4. In a separate bowl, combine both of your sugars along with the eggs.
5. Whisk them for just about a minute, not too long; you don't want too much air in the batter, otherwise your brownies may sink.
6. Add in your melted chocolate butter mixture and give it a quick whisk.
7. Add in the vanilla and stir it in.
8. Time to sift in all your dry ingredients: all-purpose flour, cocoa powder and salt.
9. Gently fold the batter until it's just combined.
10. Chop up 4–5 biscoff biscuits into eleven pieces and add those to your batter.
11. Combine them and transfer the batter to a lined 7-inch square tin.
12. Pipe or spoon some dollops of biscoff spread over the batter and swirl it around using a skewer.
13. Top that off with some more chopped biscoff biscuits.
14. Bake at 170 °C for 35 mins or until a skewer inserter comes out slightly sticky.
15. Let the brownies sit in the turned-off oven for 5 mins.
16. Remove and let them cool down at room temperature.
17. Slice into nine equal pieces using a sharp knife!

Pro Tips

1. Don't over mix the brownie batter. This is a tip that applies to most baked goods.
2. Don't over bake the brownies if you want a perfect fudge and gooey texture.

Serves: 9   **Prep time:** 15 mins   **Bake time:** 35 mins

NO-BAKE DESSERTS

RASPBERRY COCO PANNA COTTA

'This insane yet effortless dessert is just wow. Who would believe it's actually vegan?'

INGREDIENTS

For Panna Cotta

⅓ cup + 1 tbsp (100 ml) coconut milk
⅔ cup + 1 tbsp (200 ml) coconut cream
2 tbsp (25 g) sugar
1 tsp agar agar powder
½ tsp vanilla

For Raspberry Compote

1 cup (125 g) raspberries
1 tbsp (12 g) sugar
2 tsp lemon juice

STEPS

1. Grease the mould(s) of your choice.
2. Add all the ingredients for the panna cotta apart from agar agar in a saucepan.
3. Heat on medium flame and whisk to combine everything.
4. Combine the agar agar powder with 1 tbsp coconut milk and add to the pan.
5. Bring to a boil and take it away from heat.
6. Bring it to a boil once again and pour in your mould(s).
7. Let it set in the refrigerator.
8. In the meanwhile, combine all the ingredients for the compote in a pan.
9. Cook them for 7–8 mins.
10. Let it cool completely.
11. De-mould your panna cottas and pour over your prepared raspberry compote on top of them. Indulge!

Pro Tips

1. Don't boil the mixture too much otherwise your panna cotta will become hard.
2. Grease your mould(s) so that the panna cotta gets removed easily.
3. You can make one big 7–8-inch panna cotta or 4–5 small ones.

Serves: *4–5*   **Prep time:** *10 mins*   **Cook time:** *10 mins*

ULTRA-JIGGLY MATCHA PUDDING

'I knew I had to bake (or not bake in this case) at least one matcha dessert for this book, so what better than this melt-in-your-mouth matcha pudding inspired by the puddings I had during my Japan trip in 2023.'

INGREDIENTS

2 cup (500 ml) milk
¼ cup (85 g) honey
3 tbsp (24 g) cornflour
A pinch of salt
2 tsp matcha powder
½ tsp vanilla

STEPS

1. Add all the ingredients in a saucepan.
2. Whisk well to combine everything.
3. Bring to a boil over medium heat, then reduce the heat to a simmer.
4. Simmer for 4–5 mins while whisking frequently until it thickens.
5. Pour in greased moulds as desired and refrigerate for 6 hours or overnight.
6. De-mould carefully and dust with some matcha (optional).
7. Scoop into the most wonderful bite ever.

Pro Tips

1. Use the best quality of matcha that you can find; this is integral for the taste.
2. You can make this recipe vegan by using coconut milk and maple syrup.
3. Grease your moulds properly so that the pudding comes off easily.

Serves: *4–5*   **Prep time:** *5 mins*   **Cook time:** *5 mins*

BUTTERSCOTCH WALNUT BARKS

'This is probably one of the most addictive desserts from the book. You simply cannot stop at one. A friend of mine gifted me something similar a few months back which gave me the idea to come up with this.'

INGREDIENTS

1 ¼ cup (200 g) milk chocolate
1 cup (200 g) caster sugar
⅓ cup (70 g) unsalted butter
¼ tsp baking soda
½ cup (50 g) roasted walnuts
A pinch of sea salt

STEPS

1. Melt your milk chocolate using a double boiler set-up or a microwave.
2. Pour half of the quantity in a 7 x 7-inch lined tin.
3. Prepare a hard caramel by caramelizing your sugar in a saucepan. To do so, add the sugar in a saucepan and cook it on medium heat until it turns amber in colour.
4. Add in your butter a little bit at a time; be careful with this as the mixture can be extremely hot. Emulsify everything.
5. Add the baking soda, stir and pour it over the set chocolate layer.
6. Let this settle slightly and then pour over your remaining melted chocolate on top.
7. Sprinkle the roasted, chopped walnuts and a pinch of sea salt.
8. Let it set at room temperature.
9. Cut in uneven barks or just 'drop' the tin on the counter for them to break naturally.
10. That's it, now all that's left to do is to control yourself from eating too many of these.

Pro Tips

1. Use the best quality of ingredients to get this right. The fewer the ingredients, the better they need to be.
2. Make sure to not overcook or burn your caramel.
3. Add room-temperature butter, otherwise your caramel can seize.

Serves: *8–10*   **Prep time:** *5 mins*   **Cook time:** *10 mins*

STRAWBERRY CHEESECAKE MOUSSE

'This is one of the easiest, party-friendly desserts you can whip up in no time, especially when you have guests coming over. Literally anyone can make this.'

INGREDIENTS

For the Mousse
⅔ cup (150 g) non-dairy whipping cream
120 g strawberry compote
⅓ cup (75 g) cream cheese
2 tbsp (15 g) icing sugar
A dash of vanilla extract

For the Compote
¾ cup (125 g) strawberries
1 tbsp (12 g) sugar
2 tsp lemon juice

STEPS

1. Start by preparing the compote.
2. Add all the ingredients in a pan, cook on low flame for 6–7 mins. Let it cool in the fridge until it's completely chilled.
3. In a mixing bowl combine the cream cheese, icing sugar and vanilla extract. Add in your chilled compote and combine it well. Keep it aside.
4. In a separate bowl, whip up the non-dairy sweetened whipping cream to stiff peaks with the help of a beater.
5. Add in your prepared cheese mixture, then either gently cut and fold or lightly beat with your electric beater until everything is combined.
6. Transfer the mousse to a piping bag and pipe into desired serving containers.
7. Chill for a few hours and serve them to your beloved guests.

Pro Tips
1. Make sure to not deflate your whipping cream while incorporating the cheese mixture.
2. Let the mousse chill completely for the perfect taste and texture.

Serves: *4–5*   **Prep time:** *5 mins*   **Cook time:** *10 mins*

FRESH MANGO POSSET

'Mango is my favourite fruit, obviously. So, after seeing a lot of people make lemon possets and orange possets, I decided to give it a mango twist and it turned out to be the best.'

INGREDIENTS

¼ cup (100 ml) mango (Alphonso or Kesar) puree
¼ cup + 1 tbsp (50 ml) mango juice
50 g sugar (or ¼ cup) + 30 g more for the mango puree
1 cup (250 ml) cream
A pinch of salt
Zest of ½ lemon
Desiccated coconut for garnish

STEPS

1. Cut the mangoes in half and scoop them out carefully without damaging the skin. We'll use the skins to plate up our possets.
2. Blend them with 30 g of sugar to form a fine puree.
3. In a saucepan, combine cream, sugar, salt and lemon juice.
4. Start cooking on medium heat and then gradually bring to a boil. Then reduce the heat to low and let it simmer for 2 mins.
5. Then add in the mango puree and mango juice, let it simmer for 3–4 mins.
6. Continue until the mixture thickens a bit. Let it cool for a few minutes.
7. Pass this mixture through a sieve.
8. You can use the mango peels as moulds and pour the mixture in them to serve the possets.
9. Refrigerate overnight, garnish with desiccated coconut and enjoy!

Pro Tips
1. Make sure to thicken the mixture before you stop cooking it.
2. The mixture should coat the back of your spoon, that's how you know it's done.
3. You can use any kind of mangoes for this and adjust the amount of sugar accordingly.

Serves: *7–8*   **Prep time:** *10 mins*   **Cook time:** *8 mins*

CHOCOLATE ORANGE POT DE CREME

'Chocolate pairs well with mostly all kinds of fruit, but chocolate and orange are almost impossible to beat. This creamy, low-effort dessert is sure to hit the right notes.'

INGREDIENTS

⅔ cup (115 g) dark chocolate, chopped
1 cup (240 g) cream
¼ cup (50 g) caster sugar
½ tsp vanilla extract
Zest of one orange
A pinch of salt

STEPS

1. Chop your dark chocolate into small pieces, then transfer it to a bowl.
2. Set up a double boiler. Add in your cream, sugar, vanilla essence, orange zest and a pinch of salt.
3. Bring the mixture to a boil.
4. Pour this mixture over your chopped dark chocolate, let it sit for 1 min.
5. Stir everything until the chocolate has completely melted.
6. Pour this mixture into three or four ramekins or any container of your choice.
7. Refrigerate them for at least 2 hours.
8. Garnish with some orange zest and mint leaves.

Pro Tips

1. Honestly, it's so simple that you don't really need any tips, but in case the chocolate doesn't fully melt, you can microwave it for 15 seconds or just place it on a double boiler.

2. You can skip the orange zest and make a plain dark chocolate pot de creme too :)

Serves: *4–5*   **Prep time:** *5 mins*   **Cook time:** *10 mins*

LAYERED
DESSERTS

CHOCOLATE HAZELNUT PUDDING

'This is the dessert I make most of the times when I have guests arriving; it's super quick to put together and it gets the job done. I mean who doesn't love Nutella in their desserts?'

INGREDIENTS

½ cup (150 g) Nutella or any chocolate hazelnut spread
1 cup (250 g) fresh cream
25–30 biscuits of your choice
1 cup (250 ml) water
1 tbsp instant coffee

STEPS

1. Brew some coffee by combining hot water and instant coffee, let it cool completely. You could also use good-quality espresso for this.
2. Mix together Nutella/chocolate hazelnut spread and some thick fresh cream and then keep it aside.
3. Dip your biscuits in the cooled coffee for about 2–3 seconds and arrange them in a container of your choice. I have taken a 7 x 7-inch glass container.
4. Add a layer of that Nutella cream mixture.
5. Repeat these layers until both mixtures are finished.
6. Set in the fridge for 4 hours.
7. Garnish with more Nutella and some optional roasted hazelnuts and serve.

Pro Tips

1. Let your coffee cool completely, otherwise your biscuits might drown in it.
2. Make sure to use the thick portion of fresh cream from the tetra pack so that the pudding sets. This is the only crucial part to follow as there's no setting agent in this recipe.

Serves: *6–8*   **Prep time:** *10 mins*   **Cook time:** *2 mins*

FRESH STRAWBERRY TIRAMISU

'This one just teleports me back to Italy, as I first tried a fresh strawberry tiramisu there at a famous shop in Rome. That's when I thought something could even surpass a classic tiramisu. Tiramisu translated to "pick me up", and you should definitely do it with this one.'

INGREDIENTS

For the Mascarpone Filling

⅔ cup + 1 tbsp (150 g) mascarpone cheese
¼ cup (30 g) icing sugar
⅔ cup (150 g) non-dairy whipping cream
A dash of vanilla extract

For the Strawberry Compote

1 cup (150 g) strawberries
3 tbsp (42 g) caster sugar
Juice of ½ lemon

Coffee

1 cup (250 ml) of Americano

For the Layering

25–26 ladyfinger biscuits
Freeze dried strawberries for dusting (substitute with cocoa powder)

STEPS

1. Start by preparing the compote.
2. Add all the ingredients in a pan, cook on a low flame for 6–7 mins. Let it cool in the fridge until it's completely chilled.
3. Brew some Americano and let it cool. If that's not an option, then brew some instant coffee by combining hot water and instant coffee, and let it cool completely.
4. For the filling, combine the mascarpone cheese, icing sugar and vanilla extract until there are no lumps, then keep it aside.
5. In a separate bowl, whip up the non-dairy sweetened whipping cream to soft peaks using an electric beater. If you want to use dairy-based cream, make sure it's at least 35 per cent fat and in that case, gradually add ¼ cup of icing sugar while beating.
6. Add in your mascarpone mixture and gently fold everything. With that, your filling is ready.
7. For layering, dip your ladyfinger biscuits in cooled coffee and arrange them in a container.
8. Dollop half of your strawberry compote over the biscuit layer.
9. Then spread half of the mascarpone filling over it and spread evenly. Repeat all layers.
10. Refrigerate this for 6 hours or overnight.
11. Dust it with powdered freeze-dried strawberries and dig in!

Serves: 6–8   **Prep time:** 15 mins   **Cook time:** 10 mins

BLACK FOREST CREPE ROLL CAKE

'I'll be honest, I have made hundreds of desserts, but this was the first crepe cake I have ever made, and I didn't feel like making a new version, as I keep making this on repeat.'

INGREDIENTS

For the Cake
4 eggs
1 ½ cup (375 ml) milk
2 tbsp (30 ml) oil
1 cup (120 g) all-purpose flour
¼ tsp salt
2 tbsp (30 g) caster sugar
A dash of vanilla

For the Cherry Compote
150 g (1 cup) cherries (fresh or tinned)
3 tbsp (45 g) caster sugar
Juice of ½ lemon

For Layering
¾ cup or 1 tbsp (200 g) non-dairy whipping cream
⅓ cup (50 g) dark chocolate for grating

STEPS

1. Start by making the cherry compote.
2. Add all the ingredients to a pan, start cooking on a low medium flame.
3. Cook for 6–7 mins or until it gets reduced; let it cool completely. Refrigerate.
4. For the crepe batter, simply combine all the wet ingredients in a mixing bowl.
5. Then sift in your dry ingredients and whisk everything well until there are no lumps.
6. In a medium-hot non-stick pan, apply a touch of butter and add about ¼ cup of the batter. Swirl it around carefully and cook it until it gets a little colour on the bottom, then flip and cook on the other side.
7. Repeat the same with the remaining batter and you should have over a dozen crepes.
8. Arrange your crepes on top of each other while leaving about 1 cm gap in between, just like how you would spread a deck of cards on the table. Then cut all the sides so that it becomes a square in shape.
9. Whip up some non-dairy cream and spread half of it on top of the crepes.
10. Add all the cherry compote and spread it evenly. Grate half of the dark chocolate on top.
11. Then carefully but confidently roll it up, just like a Swiss roll cake, except this is much easier. And top it off with the remaining whipped cream and spread it evenly. Garnish with the remaining dark chocolate, and I'll leave the rest to your creativity :)
12. Chill it for 3–4 hours, then cut off the sides to expose those beautiful layers. Serve fresh.

Serves: *7–8*   **Prep time:** *20 mins*   **Cook time:** *25 mins*

PISTACHIO ROSE BAKLAVA

'Out of all the baklavas out there, this is probably my favourite one; it teleports you straight to Turkey and I am sure you'll make this frequently.'

INGREDIENTS

20 phyllo sheets
¼ cup (55 g) melted ghee

For the Syrup
¾ cup (150 g) sugar
¼ cup (62 g) water
2 tbsp (42 g) honey
2 cloves
¼ tsp vanilla extract
2 tsp rose water

For the Nut Mixture
1 ½ cup (180 g) shelled pistachios
½ tsp cinnamon
A pinch of grated nutmeg (optional)
A pinch of salt
2 tbsp dried rose petals

STEPS

1. Start by preparing the sugar syrup; put all the ingredients in a saucepan except for the vanilla extract and rose water.
2. Cook the mixture while stirring occasionally until it comes to a boil and then cook for a few more minutes until the syrup looks a bit thickened. Then add in the last two ingredients.
3. To prepare the nut mixture, add everything to a food processor and grind the pistachios until they come to a coarse consistency.
4. To layer the baklava, take a baking dish according to the size of your phyllo sheets, and place a parchment paper on the bottom. Grease it generously with oil/butter/ghee.
5. Place a sheet of phyllo and apply some ghee, place another sheet of phyllo, but don't apply any ghee this time. It's best to apply ghee for every alternate layer of phyllo. Repeat this step until you have five to six phyllo sheets on the bottom.
6. Add one-third of the nut mixture and spread evenly.
7. Place two or three more sheets of phyllo while applying ghee on the alternating ones.
8. Add another one-third of the nut mixture and spread evenly.
9. Place two or three more sheets of phyllo and apply ghee on the alternating ones.
10. Add the remaining of the nut mixture and spread it evenly.
11. Repeat adding five to six phyllo sheets on top while applying ghee to alternating sheets and generously apply ghee on the last top layer.
12. Cover this and refrigerate for an hour.
13. Preheat your oven to 180 °C.
14. Using a sharp knife, cut the pastry into diamond-shaped pieces (size can be as per your liking, but ideally around 1 x 1-inch squares).

Pro Tips
1. The number one thing to remember while preparing baklava is to either add cold syrup to hot baklava or hot syrup to cold baklava. This will ensure that you get the perfect crunchy texture.
2. Refrigerate the baklava before baking; this makes it easier for you to cut it without shattering those layers.
3. You can use any other nuts in this recipe and make endless variations.

Serves: 14–15   **Prep time:** 20 mins   **Bake time:** 45 mins

15. Bake in the oven at 180 °C for 40–45 mins or until a light golden colour on top.
16. Take this out of the oven and pour the cooled-down sugar syrup completely over the baklava while it is hot (make sure to do this evenly).
17. Let the baklava cool down completely and garnish with some pistachios and rose petals.

TEA
CAKES

PINEAPPLE UPSIDE-DOWN CAKE

'This is probably one of the most classic pineapple desserts and it just doesn't seem to get old. It was one of the bestsellers at my bakery.'

INGREDIENTS

For the Topping
2 tbsp (28 g) melted butter
¼ cup (50 g) brown sugar
A pinch of cinnamon

For the Cake Batter
¾ cup + 1 tbsp (190 g) curd
⅔ cup (130 g) caster sugar
1 tsp baking powder
½ tsp baking soda
⅓ cup (80 ml) oil
1 tsp pineapple extract
½ tsp vanilla extract
1 ⅓ cup (165 g) all-purpose flour
½ tsp salt

STEPS

1. Melt the brown sugar and butter in a pan until the sugar is dissolved. Pour this on a 7-inch parchment-lined cake tin.
2. Place pineapple slices and cherries creatively. Preferably use canned pineapples for this.
3. Let this sit for 5 mins.
4. Drizzle in the oil while stirring constantly; whisk it really well until no oil residue remains.
5. Add in the vanilla and pineapple extracts.
6. Sift in dry ingredients i.e. the all-purpose flour and salt.
7. Gently cut and fold the batter with a spatula, until it's just combined.
8. Pour it carefully over your topping.
9. Bake in a preheated oven at 180 °C for 35 mins or until a skewer inserted comes out clean.
10. Let it cool completely and enjoy :)

Pro Tips
1. Make sure to let the curd sit for 5 mins after you add in the leavening agents (baking powder and baking soda). This way, the baking soda reacts with the curd and you get the fluffiest cake ever.
2. Slowly add the oil while whisking so that it gets emulsified well.

Serves: *8*   **Prep time:** *20 mins*   **Bake time:** *35 mins*

CHOCOLATE WALNUT BANANA BREAD

'This bread! It's my weakness. I have two friends who love this more than anything in the world, so I keep baking it for them often, but whenever I do, I bake an extra one just for myself.'

INGREDIENTS

4 overripe bananas (5 if they are super small)

½ cup (112 g) unsalted butter

½ cup (100 g) caster sugar

½ cup (100 g) brown sugar

¼ cup (60 g) oil

3 eggs

1 ½ cup (180 g) all-purpose flour

1 tsp baking soda

1 tsp vanilla essence

¼ tsp salt

¾ cup (130 g) chocolate chips

½ cup (62 g) chopped walnuts

STEPS

1. Preheat the oven to 170 °C.
2. Then start mashing four or five overripe bananas until they look almost like a puree.
3. In a separate bowl, beat room-temperature unsalted butter, caster sugar and brown sugar for 5–6 mins or until the mixture is light and fluffy.
4. Start drizzling in your oil in a slow stream while beating constantly.
5. Add in the eggs, one at a time, and combine the batter.
6. Vanilla goes in, followed by mashed bananas. Combine everything well.
7. Sift in your dry ingredients including the all-purpose flour, baking soda and salt.
8. Gently cut and fold the mixture until it is almost combined.
9. Then add in the chocolate chips and chopped walnuts. Finish mixing until it is just combined. Transfer the batter to a 9 x 4-inch lined bread tin.
10. Top it off with some extra choco chips and/or a sliced banana as shown.
11. Bake in the preheated oven at 170 °C for 50–55 mins or until the bread springs back up when gently poked with a finger.
12. Let it cool off completely, then demould and devour.

Pro Tips

1. Don't beat the mixture too much after adding the eggs, as you don't want too much air in the batter. Otherwise, the bread might sink.

2. Bake it at 170 °C instead of the usual 180 °C, as banana bread tends to sink otherwise.

Serves: 7–8   **Prep time:** 15 mins   **Bake time:** 55 mins

DOUBLE CHOCOLATE MADELEINES

'Probably the most underrated kind of dessert. It's almost like a cake, but it has a crispier edge and a tender crumb. You can say it's a cross between a cookie and a tea cake. There's nothing else like it.'

INGREDIENTS

2 eggs

⅓ cup (65 g) caster sugar

1 tbsp (19 g) maple syrup

1 tsp vanilla extract

⅓ cup (65 g) all-purpose flour

1 tbsp + 1 tsp (20 g) cocoa powder

¼ tsp salt

¾ tsp baking powder

75 g melted butter or ⅓ cup

1 tsp orange zest

¾ cup (150 g) melted white chocolate

Pistachio for garnish (optional)

STEPS

1. Preheat the oven to 200 °C.
2. Combine the eggs, sugar and maple syrup really well. But don't beat it with an electric beater; you don't want too much air in the batter. Add in the vanilla extract and orange zest. Then combine the batter again.
3. Sift in the dry ingredients, i.e., the all-purpose flour, cocoa powder, salt and baking powder.
4. Gently fold to combine and add in the melted butter.
5. Combine the batter one last time and transfer on to a greased and dusted Madeleine sheet pan. You can use a piping bag or just scoop it using a spoon.
6. Fill the cavities until they're 80 per cent full.
7. Bake in preheated oven at 200 °C for 13–14 mins.
8. Let them cool completely and then dip them into melted white chocolate and garnish with grated pistachio.
9. Let it set and enjoy this perfect teatime snack.

Pro Tips

1. You don't need to refrigerate this batter before baking, unlike most Madeleine recipes.

2. The glaze is completely optional, but that's what makes them special :)

3. If you don't have a Madeleine pan, you can totally use this batter and bake it as cupcakes. They'll still look the same, but they won't have that iconic 'hump'.

Serves: *10–11*   **Prep time:** *15 mins*   **Bake time:** *14 mins*

GLUTEN-FREE ALMOND COCONUT ORANGE CAKE

'If you're looking for a gluten-free cake that doesn't require any chemical leavening agents, then STOP. This recipe is for you and it's just wow.'

INGREDIENTS

1 ¾ cup (175 g) almond flour
⅔ cup (66 g) desiccated coconut
¾ cup (180 g) melted unsalted butter
Zest of 1 orange
1 tsp vanilla extract
½ tsp salt
¾ cup (150 g) caster sugar
3 eggs
2 tbsp almond flakes to garnish
1 tbsp desiccated coconut flakes to garnish

STEPS

1. Preheat your oven to 180 °C.
2. Beat the eggs and sugar for 2–3 mins or until light and fluffy.
3. Add in the vanilla extract and orange zest. Combine well.
4. Slowly add the melted butter while whisking constantly.
5. Sift in the dry ingredients, including the almond flour, desiccated coconut and salt.
6. Fold them into a batter using a cut-and-fold motion. This will make sure that the air you have beaten doesn't get deflated too much.
7. Transfer the batter to a lined 8-inch cake tin. Spread evenly.
8. Garnish with almond flakes and desiccated coconut (optional).
9. Bake in a preheated oven at 180 °C for 45–50 mins or until a skewer inserted comes out clean.
10. Let it cool completely and enjoy your gluten-free treat!

Pro Tips

1. Don't whip the eggs and sugar for more than 3 mins. You don't want to incorporate too much air in the batter. Otherwise, this tea cake can sink a bit, since there's no gluten.

2. But also, don't deflate all the air you have incorporated. So cut and fold gently.

3. Let it bake completely and then let it sit in the turned-off oven for 5 mins before taking out to room temperature. This ensures the temperature drops gradually and as a result the cake doesn't sink.

Serves: 8–10   **Prep time:** 20 mins   **Bake time:** 55 mins

ADDICTIVE LEMON DRIZZLE CAKE

'This cake is probably always going to be in my list of my top three tea cakes. I can never say no to a slice of this one, especially if made using the freshest Amalfi lemons.'

INGREDIENTS

For the Cake

¾ cup + 1 tbsp (200 g) unsalted butter
1 cup (200 g) caster sugar
3 big eggs
Zest of 1 Italian lemon or 4 small regular Indian lemons
1 tsp vanilla extract
½ tsp salt
½ tsp baking powder
1 ¾ cup (220 g) all-purpose flour
⅓ cup + 2 tbsp (100 g) curd/yogurt

For the Drizzle

⅓ cup (70 g) sugar
The juice of 1 big Italian lemon or 4 small Indian lemons

STEPS

1. Preheat your oven to 170 °C.
2. Start beating the room-temperature unsalted butter with caster sugar for 5–6 mins or until perfectly light and fluffy.
3. Add in the eggs, one at a time. Combine the batter after adding each one.
4. Then add the zest of 1 big Amalfi lemon or 3–4 small Indian lemons along with vanilla extract. Combine them.
5. Sift in your dry ingredients, which includes the all-purpose flour, baking powder and salt.
6. Cut and fold, until everything is almost combined.
7. Then whisk your curd in a separate bowl until smooth and add it to your batter.
8. Combine everything one last time and transfer the batter to a 9 x 4-inch lined bread tin.
9. Pipe some butter in the middle of batter, along the length of the tin. This way you'll get a beautiful 'crack' in the middle, just like all loaf cakes do.
10. Bake in a preheated oven at 170 °C for 40–45 mins or until a skewer inserted comes out clean.
11. Prepare a glaze by combining caster sugar and lemon juice. Pour it over the cake in batches.
12. You can also poke some holes in the cake with the help of a skewer.
13. Let it cool completely and cut yourself a slice . . . thank me later.

Pro Tips

1. Use room-temperature ingredients and do not overmix the batter.
2. Use Amalfi/Italian lemons, as they are sweeter and lower in acidity; this helps in getting the perfect zingy flavour without making the cake too sour.

Serves: *8–10*   **Prep time:** *20 mins*   **Bake time:** *45 mins*

COFFEE CINNAMON CRUMBLE CAKE

'A simpler version of this cake was the bestseller at my bakery Plated By Parth, so I knew I had to take it a notch further and feature the recipe in this book. Some of the regular customers would be very happy seeing this one here.'

INGREDIENTS

For the Cake Base

1 cup (227 g) curd/yogurt
¾ cup (150 g) sugar
⅓ cup (80 ml) oil
½ tsp vanilla extract
2 tsp instant coffee
¼ tsp cinnamon
1 ½ cup (180 g) all-purpose flour
1 tsp baking powder
½ tsp baking soda
¼ tsp salt

For the Crumble Topping

⅓ cup (70 g) light brown sugar
¼ cup and 2 tbsp (45 g) all-purpose flour
1 tsp cinnamon
3 tbsp (45 g) unsalted butter, cold and cubed

STEPS

1. Make the crumble topping first by mixing all the ingredients apart from the butter in a bowl.
2. Then add the cold, chopped butter and blend it together using a pastry blender or fork. (Cold butter is easier to break down and blend with the flour without melting.)
3. When you're done, the size of the particles should be pea sized.
4. Then just refrigerate it. In the meanwhile, prepare the batter.
5. Preheat your oven to 180 °C.
6. Start by mixing your curd/yogurt and sugar until the sugar is dissolved.
7. Then slowly add in the oil while whisking constantly, followed by the vanilla extract.
8. Sift in all the dry ingredients, including the flour, baking powder, baking soda, salt, instant coffee and cinnamon. Cut and fold the batter until everything's combined.
9. Transfer to a 7-inch lined cake tin. Then sprinkle your prepared crumble on top.
10. Bake in a preheated oven at 180 °C for 35–40 mins or until a skewer inserted comes out clean. Let it cool completely and enjoy.

Serves: *8*　　　**Prep time:** *25 mins*　　　**Bake time:** *40 mins*

CHOCOLATE BATTENBERG CAKE

'The first time I made a Battenberg cake was for a brand collaboration and it went terribly wrong; not the cake, the brand deal. But on the positive side, I fell in love with this one. So will you.'

INGREDIENTS

For the Cake Batter
⅔ cup (150 g) unsalted butter
¾ cup (150 g) caster sugar
1 ¼ cup (150 g) all-purpose flour
3 eggs
1 ½ tsp baking powder
½ tsp vanilla extract
A pinch of salt
1 tbsp (15 g) milk
1 ½ tsp (7 g) cocoa powder
1 ½ tsp (7 g) milk

For the Marzipan
1 cup (100 g) almond flour
⅔ cup + 1 tbsp (80 g) icing sugar
2 tbsp (25 ml) water
60 g (3 tbsp) Nutella for spreading

STEPS

1. Start by preheating the oven to 170 °C. Cream your butter for 2 mins using a beater.
2. Add sugar and beat the mixture for 5 mins or until the mixture is light and fluffy.
3. Add in the eggs, one by one, and incorporate them as you go. Add in the vanilla.
4. Sift in the dry ingredients, which include the all-purpose flour, baking powder and salt.
5. Add in a tablespoon of milk and gently combine.
6. Divide the batter in two equal portions and add cocoa powder and milk to one of them
7. Combine the ingredients and now you have two separate batters.
8. Line a 7 x 7-inch cake tin with parchment paper and create a division in the middle with the help of parchment paper. You can form a crease in the middle to make a partition.
9. Then add the batters to two separate partitions. You can also use two separate 3.5 inch x 7-inch molds to bake the cake layers independently.
10. Then bake in a preheated oven at 170 °C for 28–30 mins or until a skewer inserted comes out clean. Then let them cool down and trim the cakes from all sides and cut them into cuboids (cut both the cakes into two long halves).
11. Prepare a marzipan by grinding almond flour and icing sugar in a food processor. After they're well combined, add in the water and grind again.

Pro Tips
1. Make sure the marzipan is completely set before rolling it out.
2. If the marzipan is too sticky, add 1 tbsp of almond flour at a time and bring it together.
3. You can use any other chocolate spread instead of Nutella or even peanut butter to stick the cake layers. Traditionally, jam is used, so that's also another option.

Serves: 7–8   **Prep time:** 40 mins   **Bake time:** 30 mins

12. After everything is mixed well, bring it all together using a spatula and if the mixture is too sticky, add some more almond flour in it. Then wrap it up in a piece of parchment paper or cling wrap and refrigerate until firm.

13. Then apply a thin layer of Nutella (or any chocolate spread) in between and join the four cake layers together so that it looks like a chessboard from the side (alternate between the colours). It should look like a long 2 x 2 Rubik's cube.

14. Dust some icing sugar on a silicon mat and roll out the firm marzipan on it until its about ¼ cm thick.

15. Then wrap the cake with the rolled-out marzipan, while making sure there are no air bubbles or cavities. Smoothen it out.

16. You can cut the open ends with a sharp knife to reveal the glorious cross section.

17. Serve this with a cup of tea or coffee and enjoy.

LAYERED
CAKES

DEATH BY CHOCOLATE CAKE

'I knew I had to include at least one of my special pure chocolate cakes in the book. By pure chocolate I mean no flavour distractions, just chocolate. This cake is everything chocolate. It's sinful, moist and creates a symphony of flavours in your mouth.'

INGREDIENTS

For the Russian Chocolate Buttercream
1 cup (226 g) unsalted butter, room temperature
1 tsp vanilla extract
¼ tsp of salt
1 cup (100 g) unsweetened cocoa powder, sifted
1 can (400 g) sweetened condensed milk

STEPS

1. Whip the room-temperature unsalted butter for 5–6 mins using an electric beater.
2. Add salt, vanilla and sifted cocoa powder. Combine on very slow speed.
3. Add the condensed milk in batches while beating on low speed.
4. Gently fold the buttercream. Refrigerate until needed.
5. For the batter, preheat your oven to 170 °C.
6. Sift the dry ingredients in a mixing bowl, including the flour, sugar, baking soda, salt and cocoa powder.
7. Then add the wet ingredients (water, oil, vinegar and vanilla) in a saucepan and bring them to a boil, add your instant coffee powder and stir it in.
8. Pour this over your dry ingredients while whisking constantly (add it while the liquid is hot).
9. Divide and transfer the batter to three lined 7-inch cake tins.
10. Bake in a preheated oven at 170 °C for 30 mins or until a skewer inserted comes out clean.
11. In the meanwhile, prepare the chocolate syrup by adding sugar and water in a saucepan.
12. Cook over medium heat until it bubbles.
13. Then remove from heat and add in the cocoa powder, whisk it really well. Let it cool down completely.
14. Now you can start assembling the cake layers.

Pro Tips

1. Let the cake cool completely before assembling the layers.
2. You can even bake the entire batter in a single tin and then trim it to end up with three separate layers. In that case, you'll have to bake it for a longer time.
3. If the buttercream is too soft, refrigerate it. If it's too hard, just leave it outside for a while.
4. You can use whichever combinations you prefer for the filling and topping.

Serves: *8–12*   **Prep time:** *1 hour 30 mins*   **Bake time:** *30 mins*

For the Chocolate Cake Sponge

1 ½ cup (180 g) all-purpose flour
1 cup (200 g) caster sugar
1 tsp baking soda
¼ cup (25 g) cocoa powder
½ tsp salt
1 cup (250 ml) water
1 tsp coffee
¼ cup + 2 tbsp (84 g) oil
1 tbsp vinegar
½ tsp vanilla extract

For the Chocolate Syrup

⅓ cup (66 g) sugar
½ cup (125 ml) water
1 tbsp (7 g) cocoa powder

For the Dark Chocolate Ganache Drip

1 cup (170 g) milk chocolate, chopped
½ cup (125 g) fresh cream
½ tsp butter
Chocolate shavings to be added while layering the cake

15. Start by applying one-third of the chocolate syrup on the first cake layer. Spread evenly.
16. Add a decent layer of the chocolate buttercream. Then grate some dark chocolate over it and any other add-ons, like chocolate chips, if your heart desires.
17. Add the next layer of the cake and repeat the same with all three layers.
18. Then cover the cake completely with the buttercream and refrigerate until set.
19. Prepare a chocolate drip by melting the milk chocolate and fresh cream together. You can do so in a microwave or using a double boiler set-up. Then stir in the butter.
20. Let it cool for a few minutes and glaze it over your set cake.
21. Refrigerate the cake again for 20 mins and top it with the remaining chocolate buttercream and all kinds of chocolate toppings you can find as shown in the picture.
22. Refrigerate one last time for about 1 hour and indulge.

ROSE LYCHEE RASPBERRY CAKE

'I would like to self-proclaim that this is one of my best cakes ever, if not the best one. In February 2024, I flew to Paris and had a very interesting flavour of Macaron—the Ispahan, a popular flavour that comprises rose, lychee and raspberry. It blew my mind, and I wondered how would that taste in a cake and ended up making this one. It's unreal!'

INGREDIENTS

For the Rose Sponge
¾ cup + 1 tbsp (190 g) curd/yogurt
⅔ cup (130 g) caster sugar
1 tsp baking powder
½ tsp baking soda
⅓ cup (80 ml) oil
2 tsp rose water
A dash of vanilla extract
A few drops of red food colour

STEPS

1. Start by preheating your oven to 170 °C.
2. Then prepare the rose cake sponge batter. Start by combining curd or yogurt, caster sugar, baking powder and baking soda in a mixing bowl. Let it rest for 5 mins.
3. The mixture would have bubbled up by now. Slowly start adding the oil while whisking constantly.
4. Then add in the rose water, vanilla extract and 1–2 drops of red food colour. Combine everything well.
5. Time to sift in the dry ingredients, which include all-purpose flour and salt.
6. Gently combine using a whisk or fold using a spatula.
7. Transfer the batter to two lined 7-inch cake tins and bake at 170 °C for 25–30 mins.
8. In the meanwhile, prepare a rose lychee syrup by heating sugar and water in a saucepan until the sugar melts. Then add the rose petals and lychee juice. Boil for 2 more mins. Let it cool completely.
9. Then prepare the raspberry compote by cooking the raspberries and sugar in a pan for 2–3 mins. Mix the cornflour and water in a separate bowl and add the slurry to the pan.
10. Stir until everything has thickened. Turn off the heat and then add the lemon juice.
11. Mix and let it cool down completely, then refrigerate until needed.

Pro Tips
1. Let all elements cool completely before assembling the cake.
2. If you're using frozen raspberries, add the remaining raspberry juice to the prepared rose lychee syrup.
3. Let the curd sit with the baking soda and powder for 5 mins; during this time the curd reacts with the soda which makes the cake super spongy as a result.

Serves: 8–12   **Prep time:** 1 hour 45 mins   **Bake time:** 30 mins

1 ⅓ cup + 1 tbsp (165 g) all-purpose flour
½ tsp salt

For the Rose Lychee Syrup

¾ cup (150 g) sugar
¾ cup (180 g) water
1 g rose petals
30 g lychee juice or 2 tbsp

For the Raspberry Compote

1 cup (100 g) fresh or frozen raspberries
3 tbsp (42 g) sugar
1tsp cornflour
1 tsp water
1 tsp lemon juice

For the White Chocolate Mousse

1 ⅓ cup (200 g) white chocolate, chopped
⅓ cup + 2 tbsp (100 g) fresh cream
1 cup (250 g) non-dairy whipping cream
A few drops of pink/red food colour

For the Toppings and Fillings

75 g of chopped lychee, plus more for garnishing
A handful of rose petals for layering and garnishing

12. Time to make the white chocolate mousse. Start by melting the chopped white chocolate and cream in a double boiler or a microwave. Let it cool completely.

13. Whip up the non-dairy sweetened whipping cream to semi-stiff peaks and gently fold in the cooled white chocolate ganache. Add in a few drops of red or pink food colour and combine. Refrigerate for 30 mins.

14. After all the elements are ready to be used, start assembling your cake.

15. Trim both the cooled cake layers from the middle to end up with four separate layers.

16. Place the first layer on the cake board and soak it with one-fourth of the rose lychee syrup.

17. Spread a thin layer of the white chocolate mousse and top it off with half of the raspberry compote.

18. Place the second cake layer on top, repeat the same steps, but instead of the compote add in chopped lychee pieces and rose petals.

19. Add in the third cake layer, followed by one-fourth of the syrup, another thin layer of the white chocolate mousse and the remaining half of raspberry compote.

20. Place the final cake layer on top, soak it with the remaining syrup and cover it with lots of white chocolate mousse.

21. Decorate the cake however you like and top it off with some rose petals, lychees and raspberries as shown.

22. Refrigerate for a few hours and slice into a piece of heaven.

RUSSIAN MEDOVIK CAKE

'This cake is probably one of the most unique desserts in the book. It has about twenty layers and although it takes a while to prepare, it definitely is a labour of love.'

INGREDIENTS

For the Cake Layers

3 cups (360 g) all-purpose flour
2 tsp baking powder
½ cup (170 g) honey or
2 tbsp (30 ml) water or
¾ cup (150 g) caster sugar or
½ cup (112 g) unsalted butter
1 tsp baking soda
½ tsp salt
1 tsp cinnamon
2 tbsp cornflour

STEPS

1. Start by prepping the dough. Sift the flour, salt, cinnamon and baking powder, and then keep it aside.
2. Cook honey in a saucepan until it starts to bubble and then take off from the heat, then add in the water. Stir to combine and add the sugar, stir completely.
3. Add in the butter and cook everything on the stove until the butter is melted.
4. Switch off the heat and then add baking soda.
5. Stir well, the mixture should become frothy, then add the cornflour and mix well.
6. Slowly add the sifted dry ingredients in batches and mix until a dough is formed.
7. Form a log, cling wrap and refrigerate for a few hours.
8. Cut into 8–10 equal dough pieces.
9. Roll them one by one on a parchment paper by sprinkling some flour and cut using a 7-inch cake ring or cookie cutter.
10. Bake them one by one in a preheated oven at 180 °C for 5 mins (don't over bake).
11. Keep covering them with cling wrap once baked.
12. Bake the excess trimmed dough similarly and grind into a coarse powder.
13. During the part where the cake dough is chilling, prepare the filling by whipping the non-dairy sweetened whipping cream to soft peaks.
14. In a separate bowl, whisk together the Greek yogurt, icing sugar and vanilla.
15. Add the yogurt mixture to the whipped cream and gently fold to combine.
16. Prepare a simple soaking syrup by combining milk and honey.

Pro Tips

1. Bake one or two layers at a time or as much as your oven can hold at a time. They will spread just a little bit so keep some gap between them.

2. Try to keep the dough and the baked layers covered at all times, especially while working on the other layers; otherwise they might dry out.

3. You can substitute the yogurt with curd but add a little extra sugar in that case.

Serves: *10–12*   **Prep time:** *1 hour 15 mins*   **Bake time:** *55–65 mins*

For the Yogurt Filling

1 ¼ cup (300 g) non-dairy sweetened cream

⅓ cup + 2 tbsp (100 g) Greek yogurt

¼ cup (30 g) icing sugar

1 tsp vanilla extract

For the Soaking Liquid

2 tbsp (30 ml) milk or 1 tbsp (21 g) honey

17. Start assembling the cake by placing the first layer on a plate or a board.
18. Brush it lightly with the soaking liquid we prepared.
19. Apply a thin layer of the yogurt filling.
20. Top it off with another cake layer and repeat all the steps until all the layers have been added.
21. Cover the cake completely with the yogurt filling.
22. Coat the entire cake with the cake crumbs which were prepared earlier.
23. Decorate the cake with the remaining yogurt filling (optional).
24. Refrigerate for a few hours or until set.

MANGO TRES LECHES CAKE

'Milk cakes have been my obsession for a few years now, but what better flavour for these than the king of fruits? Mangoes and coconut go together well here.'

INGREDIENTS

For the Cake
¾ cup + 1 tbsp (190 g) curd
⅔ cup (130 g) caster sugar
⅓ cup (80 ml) oil
1 ⅓ cup + 1 tbsp (165 g) all-purpose flour
1 tsp baking powder
½ tsp baking soda
½ tsp salt
1 tsp vanilla extract
A few drops of yellow food colour

For the Soaking Liquid
⅓ cup (80 ml) coconut milk
⅓ cup (80 g) cream
⅓ cup (100 g) condensed milk
3 tbsp (30 g) mango puree, sweetened

STEPS

1. Preheat the oven to 170 °C. Combine curd, sugar, baking powder and soda in a bowl.
2. Let it sit for 5 mins and then slowly pour in the oil while whisking constantly.
3. Then add in the vanilla extract and a few drops of yellow food colour. Mix well.
4. Sift in the dry ingredients, i.e., the all-purpose flour and salt. Gently fold to combine.
5. Transfer the batter to a lined 7-inch square cake tin and then spread evenly.
6. Bake in a preheated oven at 170 °C for 30 mins or until a skewer comes out clean.
7. Meanwhile, in a bowl combine coconut milk, cream, condensed milk and mango puree.
8. Let the cake cool down for a few minutes and then pour the entire milk mixture over it.
9. Poke a few holes in the cake if needed; this way the liquid is absorbed easily.
10. Refrigerate for 4 hours.
11. De-mould the cake and whip up the cream to soft peaks and spread it evenly on top.

Pro Tips
1. Bake one or two layers at a time or as much as your oven can hold at a time. They will spread just a little bit so keep some gap between them.
2. Try to keep the dough and the baked layers covered at all times, especially while working on the other layers; otherwise they might dry out.
3. You can substitute the yogurt with curd but add a little extra sugar in that case.

Serves: *8–12*   **Prep time:** *45 mins*   **Bake time:** *30 mins*

½ cup (120 g) non-dairy sweetened whipping cream
2 mangoes (Kesar or Alphonso)
Desiccated coconut for garnish

12. Decorate the cake with sliced mangoes as shown and top it off with desiccated coconut.
13. Trim off the edges from all four sides and optionally garnish with mint leaves.
14. Serve chilled.

Plated by Parth

ULTIMATE SALTED CARAMEL CAKE

'When I baked this one for the first time, I couldn't stop eating it, especially the caramel sauce, which I kept eating by the spoonful. All elements are that addictive; this cake in general is! The caramel ganache is out of this world.'

INGREDIENTS

For the Cake Sponge

1 ¼ cup (300 g) butter, softened, unsalted
1 ½ cup (300 g) light-brown sugar
6 eggs, large
2 ½ cup (300 g) all-purpose flour
1 tbsp baking powder
½ tsp salt
2 tsp vanilla extract

For the Caramel Ganache

½ cup (100 g) caster sugar
¼ cup (60 g) unsalted butter, room temperature
1 cup (250 g) cream, warm
½ cup (75 g) dark chocolate, chopped
¼ tsp sea salt

STEPS

1. We'll start by making the salted caramel sauce.
2. Add the sugar and water to a saucepan and bring it over a medium heat.
3. Don't mix them. Just gently swirl the pan around a couple of times so that the water gets coated over the sugar.
4. Using a wet brush apply some water on the inside of the saucepan.
5. Let it bubble until the mixture turns light golden or amber in colour.
6. Remove from heat and whisk in the cream while stirring vigorously.
7. Add the butter and let it melt in the caramel. Then heat again for 2 mins.
8. Let the caramel cool completely. Then add sea salt according to taste. Refrigerate.
9. Then prepare the ganache. In a non-stick pan, add in your caster sugar and caramelize it on medium heat. Don't stir as of yet, just shake the pan if needed.
10. Once the sugar is caramelized, add in the unsalted butter and combine it well.
11. Then add in the warm cream while whisking constantly.
12. After everything is combined, pour the hot mixture over the chopped dark chocolate and let it sit for 2 mins. Then mix everything until the chocolate is melted.
13. Lastly, add in the sea salt and mix it up. Refrigerate until needed.
14. For the cake sponge, preheat the oven to 180 °C.
15. Beat the butter and brown sugar together for 5–6 mins or until everything is light and fluffy. Then add in the eggs, one at time.

Pro Tips

1. While making the caramel, make sure to not stir with the spatula, otherwise the sugar might seize. Swirl the pan around whenever needed.
2. Use room-temperature butter and warm cream for the same, which helps avoid crystallization.
3. Use unsalted butter and adjust the salt levels as and when needed.

Serves: *10–12*   **Prep time:** *1 hour 40 mins*   **Bake time:** *40 mins*

For the Salted Caramel Sauce

¾ cup (150 g) caster sugar
2 tbsp (30 ml) water
½ cup (125 g) cream, room temperature
2 tbsp (30 g) unsalted butter, room temperature
A pinch of sea salt

For the Sugar Syrup

¾ cup (150 g) water
½ cup (125 g) sugar

For the Caramel Shards for Garnish

½ cup (100 g) caster sugar
1 ½ tbsp water

16. Time to add the vanilla extract and combine the batter.
17. Sift in the all-purpose flour, baking powder and salt. Gently fold to combine.
18. Transfer the batter to three lined 7-inch cake tins and bake at 170 °C for 35–40 mins.
19. In the meanwhile, prepare a sugar syrup by heating the sugar and water in a saucepan until it comes to boil and continue to boil it for 2 mins. Let it cool.
20. After all the elements are ready and have cooled, it's time to assemble the cake.
21. Soak the first cake layer with one-third of the sugar syrup and add a thick layer of the caramel ganache. Add a few spoons of the salted caramel and smoothen it out.
22. Then add the next layer on top and repeat the steps.
23. Coat the cake completely with the caramel ganache and let it set in the fridge for 6 hours.
24. Pipe the caramel on top of the cake so that it drips off and creates a beautiful pattern.
25. Pipe the remaining chocolate ganache on top. Refrigerate again.
26. Time to make a hard caramel. Start by cooking the sugar and water in a pan on medium heat.
27. Cook it until it turns amber in colour. And then pour it over a parchment-lined baking sheet, and let it set completely.
28. Break it off into random pieces, and with that you have your caramel shards.
29. Put the caramel shards on top of the cake and sprinkle some flaky sea salt on top.
30. Your ultimate salted caramel cake is absolutely ready. Enjoy!

WORLD'S-BEST OPERA CAKE

'This is the cake that made me open my bakery "Plated By Parth", and if I had to pick one cake for the rest of my life, it would be this one. Honestly, I can keep writing anecdotes about this one and still not get bored. But this is the cake that changed everything for me.'

INGREDIENTS

For the Joconde Sponge

3 whole eggs and 3 egg whites
2 tbsp (18 g) caster sugar
1 tbsp + 1 tsp (18 g) butter, melted
¾ cup + 2 tbsp (84 g) almond flour
⅔ cup + 1 tbsp (84 g) icing sugar
2 tbsp (18 g) all-purpose flour
A pinch of salt

For the Coffee Syrup

100 ml water
⅓ cup (60 g) sugar
4 g instant coffee

STEPS

1. Let's start by preheating the oven to 200°C.
2. Beat three whole eggs along with the almond flour and icing sugar for 7–8 mins until it becomes light and fluffy.
3. In the meanwhile, whisk three egg whites with a pinch of salt or cream of tartar (optional) until foamy, then gradually add in the caster sugar and whip till stiff peaks form.
4. Fold both the egg mixtures together, and then add your melted butter, fold that in as well. Then sift in the all-purpose flour and fold to combine.
5. Add the batter to three separate lined square cake tins (or circle) and bake in a preheated oven at 200 °C for 8–10 mins.
6. Meanwhile, heat the water and sugar in a saucepan until the water boils. Then add the instant coffee and heat for 2 more mins, and then let it cool.
7. For the ganache, heat 100 g cream and pour it over chopped dark chocolate. Let it sit for a minute and then stir until the chocolate is completely melted. Refrigerate for 3 hours.
8. For the Russian buttercream, whip the egg yolks using an electric beater until they're really creamy.
9. Then in a pan add caster sugar, water and instant coffee.

Pro Tips

1. Start by preparing the ganache first so that it sets in the fridge, followed by the syrup and buttercream. Then move on to the cake layers.

2. Traditionally, joconde sponge is baked in a sheet pan and later cut into three equal rectangular sheets for layering. So, you could do that too, but I prefer three separate cake tins.

3. After chilling the chocolate ganache, you can whip the ganache using an electric beater until it reaches stiff peaks. This is known as whipped ganache.

4. While making the buttercream, make sure to slowly pour the hot syrup over the egg yolks, otherwise the eggs can get scrambled.

Serves: *7–8*   **Prep time:** *1 hour 30 mins*   **Bake time:** *10 mins*

For the Chocolate Ganache

½ cup (100 g) dark chocolate
½ cup + 2 tbsp (100 g) cream

For the Coffee Buttercream

3 egg yolks
½ cup (90 g) caster sugar
2 tbsp (27 ml) water
1 ½ tsp coffee
¾ cup (168 g) unsalted butter

For the Chocolate Glaze

½ cup (75g) dark chocolate
⅓ cup + 2 tbsp (100 g) fresh cream

10. Keep it on medium heat and bring up the heat of the mixture until it reaches 115 °C, and then pour it slowly into the egg mixture while whisking constantly.
11. After that, start adding the unsalted butter, 1 tbsp at a time, while beating constantly.
12. Beat till it forms a nice stable buttercream, which will take a few minutes.
13. Let it cool in the fridge for a while before decorating the cake.

Assembly

1. Take one of the cake layers, and apply one-third of the coffee syrup on it. Then apply half of the coffee buttercream.
2. Add second cake layer on top of it and apply one-third of the coffee syrup. Then spread all of the chocolate ganache on it.
3. Add the third layer and apply the remaining coffee syrup on it. Then spread the remaining coffee buttercream on top.
4. Let this chill in the fridge for at least 3–4 hours or overnight.
5. Then make a glaze by melting the chocolate and cream together. Let it cool for 10 mins and pour it over the cake. Let it cool completely.
6. Trim off all four sides of the cake to reveal the beautiful cross section of the cake.
7. Optionally write 'opera' on top of the cake/pastries using leftover chocolate ganache and take a bite of the best cake in the world.

BAKING BREAD

CHEESY KOREAN GARLIC BUNS

'This is the bread my family has loved the most by far, including my close friends. I have baked over seventy-eighty varieties of breads over the years, but this one is unbeatable.'

INGREDIENTS

For the Cream Cheese Filling

1 ¾ cup (400 g) cream cheese, softened
⅓ cup + 2 tbsp (100 g) cream
⅓ cup (65 g) caster sugar

For the Garlic Butter Custard

3 tbsp + 1 tsp (50 ml) milk
1 tbsp (8 g) cornflour
½ cup (113 g) unsalted butter, melted
1 tbsp or 2 tsp (30 g) condensed milk
1 tbsp (20 g) honey
115 g garlic cloves, chopped
¼ tsp salt
Coriander leaves or parsley for garnish

For the Assembly

8 buns of choice
Parmesan cheese for grating on top

STEPS

1. Combine the cream cheese, cream and caster sugar using a whisk and keep it aside.
2. In a saucepan, add melted butter and chopped garlic cloves.
3. Cook for 2 mins, and then add in the condensed milk, salt and honey. Combine.
4. Prepare a cornflour slurry by mixing cornflour with water and add that to the pan.
5. Cook this mixture until it is slightly thickened and then add chopped parsley in it.
6. Let it cool off for 15 mins.
7. Preheat the oven to 190 °C.
8. Take your buns and slit them three to four times up to 70 per cent of the way vertically, so that you end up with six to eight segments when viewed from the top—similar to how you would look at a pizza. But make sure to not slit them all the way. The bottom should still be intact.
9. Using a piping bag, fill the cream cheese filling in the cavities, generously.
10. Dunk the buns in the cooled garlic butter custard, while holding them upside down.
11. Then place them on a lined baking sheet, grate some parmesan cheese on top and bake in a preheated oven at 190 °C for 20–25 mins.
12. Grate some more parmesan on top and sprinkle some freshly chopped parsley as well.
13. Pipe a dollop of the cream cheese mixture in the middle to end the plating.
14. With this, you have just made the most soul-satisfying bread of all time.

Pro Tips

1. You can use any buns for this or follow the measurements from my maritozzo recipe.
2. You can adjust the flavours as per your liking, for e.g., the quantity of garlic used.

Serves: *8*　　　**Prep time:** *45 mins*　　　**Bake time:** *25 mins*

CHEESY PARMESAN GARLIC KNOTS

'I think this could be the easiest bread recipe ever and if you're a budding baker, scared to work the dough, this could be the easiest start.'

INGREDIENTS

For the Dough

3 ⅓ cup (400 g) or all-purpose flour or bread flour

8 g salt

½ tsp instant yeast

1 cup (250 g) lukewarm water

For the Garlic Butter

50 g garlic cloves, chopped

3 tbsp (50 g) unsalted butter

A handful of chopped parsley

25 g grated parmesan cheese

STEPS

1. Mix flour and salt, keep aside.
2. Mix lukewarm water with instant yeast and let it sit for 3–4 mins.
3. Add the yeast water to your flour in three to four batches and mix everything using a spatula.
4. Switch to your hands and mix until all of the flour is hydrated.
5. Let this sit for 15 mins. Knead for 3–4 mins.
6. Rest for 15 mins. Knead for 2 more mins.
7. Cover with cling wrap and keep at room temperature for 2 hours or until the dough has doubled in size.
8. Deflate the air from the dough and divide in equal balls of 50 g each. You could also eyeball it and divide them into 12–13 balls.
9. Roll each ball into a cylinder and then tie it into a knot as shown.
10. Place all of them on a lined baking sheet and cover. Let them proof for 35–40 mins.
11. Meanwhile, make the garlic butter by heating some unsalted butter in a pan until it has melted.
12. Add in the chopped garlic and cook for 2 more mins.
13. Add in the chopped parsley and grated parmesan. Stir to combine and take it off heat.
14. Preheat the oven to 200 °C.
15. After the knots are proved, brush them with the garlic butter and bake for 15 mins or until they look golden brown.
16. Brush them generously once again with some garlic butter.
17. Sprinkle freshly grated parmesan cheese to finish the plating.

Pro Tips

1. *If you're using active dry yeast, then use a heaping ½ tsp instead of just ½ tsp yeast and after adding it to the lukewarm water, let it bloom/foam first.*

2. *Kneading this dough isn't tricky, but if it feels difficult, just let it rest for 5 mins.*

Serves: *12–13*   **Prep time:** *30 mins*   **Proofing time:** *2 hour 40 mins*   **Bake time:** *15 mins*

CHOCOLATE HAZELNUT BOMBOLINIS

'These ultra-fluffy chocolaty bombolinis will surely fulfil all your cravings. They're just wow.'

INGREDIENTS

For the Dough

½ cup + 2 tbsp (155 g) milk

1 egg

2 tbsp (25 g) caster sugar

2 cup + 2 tbsp (255 g) all-purpose flour

¾ tsp heaped instant yeast

½ tsp salt

¼ cup (60 g) unsalted butter

Oil for frying

½ cup (100 g) caster sugar for coating

350 g chocolate hazelnut spread for filling

STEPS

1. We'll start by combining the all-purpose flour, caster sugar, instant yeast and salt in a mixing bowl.
2. Then we'll combine the milk and egg in a separate bowl.
3. Add the liquid ingredients to the wet ingredients in batches and combine them.
4. Start kneading the dough with your hands or a stand mixer.
5. After kneading the dough for 4–5 mins, it should stop sticking to your hands completely.
6. Then start adding the butter, 1 tbsp at a time, and combine it well.
7. After adding all of the butter, knead the dough until it turns completely smooth and passes the windowpane test, which means that when you gently stretch a small chunk of the dough, it should form a thin, translucent membrane without tearing (like a windowpane).
8. Then shape it into a ball and place it in a lightly oiled bowl.
9. Cover with cling film and refrigerate overnight.
10. De-gas and roll it out into a thick sheet (around ½–¾-inch thick).
11. Then cut as many circles out of it as possible using a 3½–4-inch cookie cutter.
12. Cut a sheet of parchment paper into smaller pieces and place all the dough balls on a parchment paper each. Keep them all on a baking sheet and cover for 45–50 mins.
13. Fifteen mins before frying, preheat the oil at medium heat and wait until it reaches 180 °C.
14. Fry two or three bombolinis at a time at a temperature range of 170–80 °C. Flip halfway.
15. Once they're golden colour on both sides, gently drain the excess oil and place them on a wire rack.
16. Let them cool completely and then coat them in caster sugar.
17. Poke a hole carefully and fill them generously with any chocolate hazelnut spread.
18. Serve fresh and devour them.

Pro Tip

1. You can make regular doughnuts using the same dough and glaze them too.

Serves: *12–14* **Prep time:** *40 mins* **Proofing time:** *24 hours (in the fridge)* **Cook time:** *20 mins*

WHITE CHOCOLATE PISTACHIO BABKA

'I baked my first-ever babka during the pandemic; of course it was a chocolate version. But ever since I have eaten and made so many more flavours, still nothing comes close to this pistachio babka that just hits the right notes.'

INGREDIENTS

For the Dough
1 ½ cup + 3 tbsp (270 g) all-purpose flour
¼ cup (50 g) caster sugar
½ tsp (5 g) instant yeast
88 g water
2 small eggs
Approx. 5 tbsp (75 g) unsalted butter, at room temperature
½ tsp salt

For the Syrup
3 tbsp (45 ml) water
3 tbsp (40 g) or sugar

STEPS

1. Mix the dry ingredients—all-purpose flour, sugar, instant yeast and salt—in a stand mixer bowl, then slowly add the water and keep mixing. You can also use your hands or a spatula for the same.
2. Then add in the eggs, knead until this forms a dough.
3. Start adding the butter, 1 tbsp at a time. Knead for 7–8 more mins or until you reach a windowpane consistency.
4. Transfer the dough to a greased bowl, cling wrap and refrigerate overnight.
5. Next day, de-gas and roll the dough into a ½-inch-thick square and spread your pistachio filling evenly (recipe below).
6. Roll into a tight log and refrigerate it for a few minutes or until it hardens up.
7. Cut lengthwise, while keeping one end intact, and shape into a spiral or a braid.
8. Transfer it to a 9 x 4½-inch lined loaf tin and cover and proof for 1 hour 15 mins–1 hour 30 mins or until doubled.
9. Bake in a preheated oven at 190 °C for 30 mins or golden brown on top.
10. Prepare a sugar syrup by cooking water and sugar in a saucepan. Cook for 1–2 mins and then brush the babka with this syrup right after it's out of the oven.
11. Let it cool and serve.

Pro Tips

1. You can prepare the dough and pistachio filling on Day 1 and then shape the bread and bake it the next day.

2. If you want to make the bread in a day, you can choose to do a normal fermentation instead of a cold fermentation. Just let the dough ferment at room temperature for 1 ½ hours–2 hours or until it has doubled in size.

3. You can make this recipe using any other nuts as well, but pistachios just hit the right spot.

Serves: *10–12* **Prep time:** *1 hour 15 mins* **Proofing time:** *24 hours (in the fridge)* **Bake time:** *15 mins*

For the Pistachio Filling

¾ cup (100 g) pistachios, unsalted and shelled
⅔ cup (100 g) white chocolate
2 ½ tbsp (40 g) unsalted butter
A pinch of salt

STEPS

1. Bring some water to a boil, then add in the pistachios and cover.
2. Turn off the heat and let them sit for 4 mins.
3. Transfer them to ice-cold water.
4. Peel the pistachios or rub them between a cloth so that the skin comes off.
5. Melt the butter and white chocolate using a double boiler or a microwave.
6. Blend the pistachios to a nice purée. Add the cooled chocolate butter mixture and a pinch of salt.
7. Blend again briefly until smooth.
8. Refrigerate for a few hours or overnight.

ASSORTED MARITOZZO

'Maritozzo was one of the many revelations I had during my Italy trip in 2024. I felt it's kinda like a doughnut but also like a cream bun. But it's so much more and different. Unique!'

INGREDIENTS

For the Dough

2 cups (250 g) T55 bread flour
¼ cup (50 g) sugar
3 ½ g instant dry yeast
½ cup (125 ml) milk
2 tbsp (35 g) oil
1 tsp vanilla extract
Lemon zest or orange zest
A pinch of salt

For the Pastry Cream

1 cup (250 ml) milk
2 tbsp (25 g) sugar
1 tsp vanilla extract
4 tsp cornstarch
A pinch of salt
1–2 drops yellow colour (optional)

STEPS

For the Dough

1. Combine T55 flour, sugar, instant yeast and salt in a mixing bowl.
2. Add in vanilla extract, milk, oil and lemon zest (you can also use orange zest for a variation).
3. Combine everything using a dough whisk, your hands or a spatula.
4. Knead the dough for 8–10 mins using hands or a stand mixer.
5. The dough should become completely smooth.
6. Shape the dough into a ball and place it in a greased bowl. Cover with cling film.
7. Refrigerate it overnight and next day, punch out all the air.
8. Divide the dough into five equal portions and shape them into an oblong or cylindrical shape.
9. Place them on a lined baking sheet and let them proof for an hour or until they're almost double in size.
10. Brush the maritozzo with milk and bake in a preheated oven at 180 °C for 15 mins or until light golden in colour.
11. Let them cool completely and cut them three-fourth of the way, then fill with diplomat cream all the way. (Recipe below.)
12. Dip them in various assortments of toppings, such as chopped pistachios, cranberries, chocolate chips and hazelnuts. Or leave them plain if that's how you like it.
13. Dust them with icing sugar and serve fresh.

Pro Tips

1. You can use other fillings, such as regular whipped cream if you want a simpler cream bun.
2. You can make assorted maritozzos by changing the toppings as you like or just make the classic vanilla ones, dusted with some icing sugar.
3. Consume them fresh as they're not meant to be stored for too long.
4. It's best to use T55 bread flour for the best results, but if you can't find it, you can use regular all-purpose flour too.

Serves: 5   **Prep time:** *1 hour 15 mins*   **Proofing time:** *24 hours (in the fridge)*   **Bake time:** *15 mins*

For the Diplomat Cream

Prepared pastry cream

½ cup (125 g) non-dairy sweetened whipping cream

For the Pastry Cream

1. Reserve 2 tbsp of milk and add the remaining to a saucepan, along with the sugar, salt and vanilla extract.
2. Cook on a medium heat, while stirring constantly, for about a minute.
3. Then make a slurry using the extra milk and cornflour and add it to your milk mixture.
4. Cook at a low medium flame until the mixture thickens and coats the back of your spoon or spatula.
5. You could also add a drop of yellow food colour to give it the classic colour of pastry cream, but that's optional.
6. Cling wrap and chill until needed.

For the Diplomat Cream

1. Whip up some non-dairy sweetened whipping cream to soft peaks.
2. Add in the cooled pastry cream and gently fold them together.
3. With that, the diplomat cream is ready.

NO-KNEAD ASSORTED FOCACCIA MUFFINS

'If I had to introduce someone to bread baking, I'd probably teach them this recipe first. I can't even count how many times I have prepared various kinds of focaccias using this base recipe. It's literally the easiest and most low-effort, yet epic recipe.'

INGREDIENTS

For the Dough
2 cups (250 g) all-purpose flour
1 tsp sea salt
1 tsp instant yeast
Little less than 1 cup (225 ml) water
2–3 (30 g) tbsp olive oil

For the Topping
Grated parmesan cheese
A few slices of olives
½ red bell pepper
1–2 sun-dried tomatoes, chopped
5–6 slices of jalapeños
Pizza seasoning for sprinkling

STEPS

1. Combine the flour, salt and yeast in a mixing bowl.
2. Then gradually add in your water while mixing the dough using a spatula or your hands.
3. Keep mixing for 2 mins, no need to knead.
4. Then add in the olive oil and mix again.
5. Cover with cling wrap and refrigerate overnight.
6. The next day, punch out all the air and divide the dough into six equal pieces.
7. Line a muffin tray with parchment papers or cupcake liners.
8. Drizzle a little olive oil in each liner, followed by a sprinkling of sea salt.
9. Place the dough balls in the cupcake liners, cover and let them double in size at room temperature. This should take about 45 mins.
10. Dip your fingers in olive oil and gently poke the doughs and 'dimple' them.
11. Now's the fun part. Top each of them with different toppings of your choice.
12. I went with parmesan cheese, jalapeños, bell peppers, olives and sun-dried tomatoes.
13. Bake in a preheated oven at 190 °C for 25 mins or until golden on top.
14. Let them cool for 10 mins and enjoy.

Pro Tips
1. You can use the same recipe and bake a full-sized focaccia as well. Just don't divide it.
2. Play around with more fun toppings like oregano, chillies, zaatar and garlic.

Serves: 6   **Prep time:** *30 mins*   **Proofing time:** *24 hours (in the fridge)*   **Bake time:** *25 mins*

CUPCAKES AND MUFFINS

TRIPLE CHOCOLATE MUFFINS

'Imagine walking in a kitchen and getting surprised with the aroma of these super-moist chocolaty muffins in the oven. Any chocolate lover would go crazy after having them.'

INGREDIENTS

1 cup (140 g) all-purpose flour

¼ cup + 2 tbsp (37 g) unsweetened cocoa powder

1 tsp baking powder

¼ tsp baking soda

¼ tsp salt

½ cup + 2 tbsp (125 g) caster sugar

1 large egg

½ cup + 2 tbsp (150 ml) milk

2 tsp vinegar

2 tbsp (30 g) melted butter

2 tbsp (30 ml) oil

1 tsp instant coffee

1 teaspoon vanilla extract

¼ cup chocolate chips

¼ cup dark chocolate chunks

STEPS

1. Preheat the oven to 190 °C.
2. Start by whisking the eggs and caster sugar using a balloon whisk until well combined.
3. Then prepare buttermilk by combining milk and vinegar. Add it to your eggs.
4. Gradually add the melted butter and oil while whisking constantly.
5. Add in the vanilla extract and mix again.
6. Sift in the dry ingredients: the all-purpose flour, cocoa powder, baking powder, baking soda, coffee and salt.
7. Gently fold the batter until it's just combined.
8. Then add in lots of chocolate chunks and chocolate chips.
9. Scoop the batter in a muffin tray lined with muffin liners. Fill them till the batter is at 80 per cent height of the liners.
10. Top them off with a few extra chocolate chips/callets.
11. Bake in a preheated oven at 190 °C for 25–30 mins or until a skewer inserted comes out clean.
12. Let them cool off for a just a while and then indulge while they're warm.

Pro Tips

1. Don't over mix the batter at any stage, otherwise the muffins won't be fluffy enough.
2. You can add more chocolate if your heart desires; no one's judging :)

Serves: 6   **Prep time:** *30 mins*   **Bake time:** *30 mins*

DULCE DE LECHE CUPCAKES

'Centre filled with a caramel-like filling, these cupcakes are sure to surprise everyone who's got a sweet tooth. Best part is that this recipe requires no eggs, no butter—just love.'

INGREDIENTS

For the Cupcakes
⅔ cup (180 ml) curd
½ cup (100 gm) sugar
⅓ tsp baking soda
⅔ tsp baking powder
⅓ cup (80 ml) oil
1 tsp vanilla extract
1 cup (120 g) all-purpose flour
A pinch of salt

For the Dulce de Leche
400 g can sweetened condensed milk

For the Topping and Filling
Dulce de leche
150 g non-dairy sweetened whipping cream

STEPS

1. Remove the label of the condensed milk can.
2. Place it in a pressure cooker and fill the cooker with water. The can should be completely submerged, and the water should be a few inches above the can level.
3. Then close the lid and let it cook at medium flame until the first whistle goes off.
4. Lower the flame and let it cook for 15–17 mins more.
5. Turn off the flame and let the cooker depressurize naturally. This will take at least an hour.
6. Let the can come down to room temperature as well. Then refrigerate.
7. Carefully open the can and you have just made yourself an easy and delicious dulce de leche.
8. Preheat the oven to 170 °C. Combine the curd, sugar, baking powder and soda in a bowl.
9. Let it sit for 5 mins and slowly pour in the oil while whisking constantly.
10. Then add in the vanilla extract. Mix well.
11. Sift in the dry ingredients, i.e., the all-purpose flour and salt. Gently fold to combine.
12. Transfer the batter to a cupcake tray lined with cupcake liners.
13. Bake in a preheated oven at 170 °C for 25–30 mins or until a skewer comes out clean.
14. For assembly, scoop out the centre portion of your cupcakes using an apple corer or a tablespoon. Fill them generously with dulce de leche.
15. Whip up the non-dairy cream to stiff peaks and pipe it over your cupcakes.
16. Pipe some more dulce de leche on top of the cream to finish the plating. Chill and serve.

Serves: *10*   **Prep time:** *45 mins*   **Bake time:** *30 mins*

VANILLA BEAN CUPCAKES

'These cupcakes = pure nostalgia. Easy to make, and so yum, especially when made with real vanilla pods.'

INGREDIENTS

For the Batter
⅔ cup (180 ml) curd
½ cup (100 g) sugar
⅓ cup (80 ml) oil
1 pod or 1 tsp vanilla extract
1 cup (120 g) all-purpose flour
A pinch of salt
⅓ tsp baking soda
⅔ tsp baking powder

Vanilla Russian Buttercream
¾ cup (170 g) unsalted butter, room temperature
⅓ cup (100 g) condensed milk
1 pod of vanilla or 1 tsp vanilla extract
A pinch of salt

STEPS

1. Preheat the oven to 170 °C. Combine the curd, sugar, baking powder and soda in a mixing bowl.
2. Let it all sit for 5 mins so that the curd and soda can react. Then slowly pour in the oil while whisking constantly.
3. Then cut open a pod of vanilla and scrape out the vanilla beans. Add them to the batter and stir well.
4. Sift in the dry ingredients: the all-purpose flour and salt. Gently fold everything to combine.
5. Transfer the batter to a cupcake tray lined with cupcake liners.
6. Bake in a preheated oven at 170 °C for 25–30 mins or until a skewer comes out clean.
7. Meanwhile, prepare the Russian buttercream.
8. Whip the room-temperature unsalted butter for 5–6 mins using an electric beater.
9. Add the condensed milk while beating on low speed.
10. Add in a pinch of salt and vanilla beans from an entire vanilla pod.
11. Fold the buttercream gently. Refrigerate until needed.
12. Let the cupcakes cool off completely and pipe them with the glorious buttercream.

Pro Tips
1. You can substitute the vanilla pod with vanilla extract (or essence), but pods are ideal.
2. Use room-temperature ingredients to get the best results.

Serves: *10*   **Prep time:** *35 mins*   **Bake time:** *30 mins*

CARROT WALNUT CUPCAKES

'My favourite type of frosting has to be with cream cheese and when that's paired with these carrot walnut cupcakes, they create magic.'

INGREDIENTS

For the Batter

1 cup (70 g) all-purpose flour

¾ cup (80 g) caster sugar

40 g walnuts

¼ tsp cinnamon

A pinch of salt

¼ tsp baking powder

¼ tsp baking soda

1 egg

⅓ cup (75 ml) oil

62 g carrots, grated

½ tsp vanilla extract

For the Cream Cheese Frosting

90 g cream cheese

35 g icing sugar

½ tsp vanilla extract

90 g nondairy whipping cream

STEPS

1. Preheat the oven to 180 °C.
2. Start by whisking sugar and egg until combined.
3. Then slowly add the oil while whisking constantly.
4. Next, add in the grated carrots and vanilla. Combine them well.
5. Sift in the dry ingredients: the all-purpose flour, baking powder, baking soda, cinnamon and salt.
6. Gently fold the batter until everything just barely comes together.
7. Lastly, add some chopped roasted walnuts. Fold one last time.
8. Scoop the batter in a cupcake tray lined with cupcake liners.
9. Bake in a preheated oven at 180 °C for 20 mins or until they spring back up when pressed.
10. Meanwhile, prepare the cream cheese frosting. Start by combining the cream cheese and icing sugar in a mixing bowl until there are no lumps. Then add the vanilla.
11. In a separate bowl, whip up the non-dairy sweetened whipping cream to stiff peaks.
12. Add in the cream cheese mixture and gently fold to combine.
13. Once the cupcakes are cooled, frost them as you like and garnish with walnuts or fondant carrots. Fondant carrots are totally optional, and honestly the cupcakes taste better without them, but things you do for plating :)

Serves: *8*   **Prep time:** *35 mins*   **Bake time:** *20 mins*

CHEESECAKES

BURNT BASQUE CHEESECAKE

'The easiest baked cheesecake of all time. This San Sebastián style-inspired cheesecake is never a miss. When I started posting this eggless version, so many people started asking me to restart my bakery just so that they can order it. I had to host a bake sale just for this. We sold too many cheesecakes that day.'

INGREDIENTS

For the Batter

2 cups (450 g) cream cheese
¼ cup (50 g) caster sugar
2½ tbsp (18 g) all-purpose flour
5 g cornflour
¾ cup + 2 tbsp (220 g) fresh cream
½ cup (150 g) condensed milk
1 tsp vanilla extract
Zest of 1 lemon

For the Glaze

1 cup (150 g) milk chocolate
Oil as needed

STEPS

1. Preheat the oven to 230 °C.
2. In a bowl, add in room-temperature cream cheese and caster sugar.
3. Combine them until the sugar is dissolved.
4. Into this, add in condensed milk and combine it as well.
5. In a separate bowl, combine cream and flour until there are no lumps.
6. Then add the cream and flour mixture to the cream cheese mixture along with the zest of a small lemon and vanilla extract.
7. Fold everything until well combined.
8. Transfer the batter to a 5–6-inch round cake tin lined with parchment paper.
9. Bake in the preheated oven at 230 °C for about 30 mins or until the top looks 'burnt', or browned, while the centre is still jiggly.
10. Let it cool down completely. You can serve it either at room temperature or after cooling it in the fridge for a few hours.
11. For the glaze, just melt the milk chocolate in a double boiler or microwave. Add a few spoons of any neutral oil (any flavour-less or odourless oil) to it and combine until you get the desired consistency.

Pro Tips

1. You can substitute the vanilla with real vanilla pod for an even better taste.
2. I like to let the cheesecake (all of them in general) sit in the turned off oven after baking, for about 5 mins to let the temperature drop gradually, this helps to avoid any sinking.
3. If you have a fan option in your oven, turn it on. It really helps in getting the perfect colour on top.

Serves: *6–8*   Prep time: *20 mins*   Bake time: *30 mins*

BAKED CAPPUCCINO CHEESECAKE

'Inspired by my bestseller classic baked cheesecake, this one is a dream come true for all the coffee lovers and quite possibly my favourite one in this book. It's heaven in each bite.'

INGREDIENTS

For the Crust

120 g chocolate biscuits, melted

70 g butter, melted

For the Batter

1 cup + 2 tbsp (250 g) cream cheese

¾ cup (150 g) caster sugar

3 eggs

½ cup (125 g) fresh cream

1 tbsp instant coffee

2 tbsp (30 g) curd

Zest of 1 lemon

1 tsp vanilla extract

1 tbsp cornflour

For the Coffee Ganache

⅔ cup (100 g) milk chocolate

3 tbsp + 1 tsp (50 g) cream

2 tsp coffee

STEPS

1. Heat the fresh cream until it's warm, either in a microwave or a double boiler. Then add in the instant coffee. Mix well and let it cool. Preheat the oven to 160 °C.
2. Grease your spring foam cake tin with butter and cover the sides with parchment paper.
3. Grind all of the biscuits into a coarse consistency, preferably using a rolling pin or a food processor. Don't grind them all the way.
4. Then add in the melted butter. Mix both of them nicely to get a wet sand consistency.
5. Transfer this to the lined cake tin and form a crust for the cheesecake using a measuring cup or a spoon. Refrigerate the crust for 15–20 mins. Meanwhile, prepare the batter.
6. Take your cream cheese and caster sugar. Mix them well. Then add one egg at a time and mix the batter to combine the eggs.
7. To the bowl containing your coffee cream mixture, add in the cornflour and mix them very well, ensuring no lumps remains. Add the vanilla extract and zest of a lemon.
8. Add this cream mixture to your batter and combine everything.
9. Strain and pour this batter in your crust. Prepare a water bath and bake in a preheated oven at 160 °C for 45–55 mins. Let it cool in the fridge overnight before de-moulding.
10. Prepare a coffee ganache by heating your cream in a double boiler until it's warm, then add in the coffee and stir well. Add in the chocolate and mix everything until melted. Let it set and then spread it evenly over your cheesecake and cut a slice. Serve fresh.

Pro Tips

1. Use room temperature ingredients and prepare a water batch to ensure that your cheesecake doesn't crack.

2. Strain the batter to get a perfectly smooth texture.

Serves: *8*　　　**Prep time:** *45 mins*　　　**Bake time:** *55 mins*

NO-BAKE PEACH CHEESECAKE

'Freshness in each bite—that's how I'd like to describe this cake. Blueberry, strawberry, classic and chocolate, these are the only flavours that typically come to mind when you think of cheesecakes. Well, not any more!'

INGREDIENTS

For the Peach Compote
1 ⅓ cup + 2 tbsp (225 g) peach
⅓ cup (66 g) sugar
2 tsp cornflour + 2 tsp water
3 tbsp (45 ml) water
Few squeezes of lemon juice

For the Crust
120 g biscuits
5 tbsp (70 g) butter, melted

For the Batter
110 g peach compote (remaining for topping)
¼ cup (30 g) icing sugar
⅔ cup + 1 tbsp (160 g) cream cheese
⅔ cup + 1 tbsp (160 g) non-dairy sweetened whipping cream
A dash of vanilla

STEPS

1. Prepare the compote by cooking the chopped peaches and sugar in a pan for 5 mins or until softened. Then prepare a cornflour slurry by combining cornflour with water. Add that and stir. Add more water as needed and let it thicken. Add lemon juice, turn off the heat and let this chill completely.
2. Line your 7-inch springform cake tin with parchment and prepare the crust by combing crushed digestive biscuits and melted butter. Transfer to the tin and press firmly.
3. Refrigerate the tin while your prep the batter. Start by combining room temperature-softened cream cheese with icing sugar. Keep mixing until there are no lumps.
4. Then add in the peach compote and vanilla extract. Combine well.
5. In a separate bowl, whip up non-dairy sweetened whipping cream to stiff peaks and gently fold both the mixtures together. With that the filling is ready.
6. Pour this in your prepared crust and carefully spread it evenly, while ensuring that no air bubbles are formed. Tap it on the counter and refrigerate overnight.
7. De-mould and top it off with the remaining peach compote and serve fresh.

Pro Tips
1. *You can use fresh or frozen peaches for this; it tastes amazing both ways.*
2. *You can blend the peach compote, which you're adding in the batter for a smoother feel.*

Serves: *8*   **Prep time:** *50 mins*

RED VELVET OMBRE CHEESECAKE

'This cheesecake is surely a great cross between cakes and cheesecakes. You don't have a crust; you have a super-moist cake base instead with a beautiful cheesecake on top.'

INGREDIENTS

For the Cake Layers

½ cup (60 g) all-purpose flour
1 tsp cocoa powder
¼ tsp baking soda
¼ tsp salt
⅓ cup (80 ml) milk
1 tsp vinegar
3 tbsp (40 ml) oil
⅓ cup (65 g) sugar
½ tsp vanilla extract
¼ tsp red food colour
½ tsp vinegar

For the Cheesecake Filling

¾ cup + 2 tbsp (200 g) cream cheese, room temperature
⅓ cup (40 g) icing sugar
1 tsp vanilla
¾ cup + 1 tbsp (200 g) non-dairy sweetened whipping cream
A few drops of red food colour

STEPS

1. Preheat your oven to 160 °C.
2. Make buttermilk by combining the milk and 1 tsp vinegar.
3. Add in the oil, sugar, vanilla, a few drops of red food colour and vinegar. Mix well.
4. Sift in the all-purpose flour, cocoa powder, baking soda and salt. Gently fold to combine.
5. Transfer the batter to a 7-inch lined cake tin and bake at 160 °C for 25 mins or until a skewer inserted comes out clean. Trim the cake from the centre to get two layers.
6. For the filling, combine the cream cheese, icing sugar and vanilla, then keep it aside.
7. Then whip up some non-dairy sweetened whipping cream to stiff peaks. Cut and fold both the mixtures, then divide the filling into four equal portions. Colour them in four different ratios using red food colour. So that you achieve with four different shades: white, light pink, pink and red. Then cover one of the cake layers with a thick plastic sheet or mould.
8. Then add the coloured fillings one at a time, while spreading evenly and tapping after each addition to avoid any air bubbles. This will create an ombre effect.
9. Top it off with an optional final layer of whipped cream. Refrigerate overnight
10. Then garnish with red velvet cake crumbs made with the second cake layer.
11. Carefully de-mould or remove the plastic sheet and smoothen the sides using an offset spatula to achieve a smooth ombre effect.

Serves: 8   **Prep time:** 60 mins   **Bake time:** 25 mins

TRIPLE CHOCOLATE CHEESECAKE

'This is surely a chocolate lovers' dream come true. I wanted to call this a chocolate overload cheesecake, as it has chocolate oozing out of each element.'

INGREDIENTS

For the Ganache
⅔ cup (100 g) dark chocolate
3 tbsp + 1 tsp (50 g) cream

For the Crust
120 g chocolate biscuits
5 tbsp (70 g) melted butter

For the Filling
⅔ cup + 1 tbsp (120 g) melted dark chocolate
¼ cup (30 g) icing sugar
⅔ cup + 1 tbsp (160 g) cream cheese
⅔ cup + 1 tbsp (160 g) non-dairy sweetened whipping cream
A dash of vanilla
30 g dark chocolate shavings

STEPS

1. Start by preparing a dark chocolate ganache. Heat the cream in a double boiler or a microwave for 2 mins and then add in your dark chocolate. Let it melt then chill.
2. For the crust, start by lining a 7-inch spring form cake tin. Then crush your chocolate biscuits with the help of a rolling pin and zip lock bag. You can also use a grinder.
3. Then add some melted butter to it and combine. Transfer this to your cake tin and press firmly to form the crust, then refrigerate until needed.
4. For the filling, combine cooled melted chocolate with cream cheese, icing sugar and vanilla extract. Mix everything well and keep it aside.
5. Whip up the non-dairy sweetened whipping cream to stiff peaks and fold both the mixtures gently. Then pour this over your prepared crust in batches and spread evenly.
6. Smoothen it out and give a few taps on the counter to release air bubbles.
7. Then refrigerate for 6 hours or up to overnight. Pipe the chocolate ganache over it and garnish with some dark chocolate shavings.
8. Slice and enjoy.

Pro Tips
1. Make sure to use good dark chocolate for all the recipes in the book, as it can make or break your desserts.
2. If you are using chocolate biscuits with a cream filling, just remove the cream and add it to your cream cheese mixture. Then combine really well to eliminate any lumps.
3. You can use a cake ring or a plastic sheet to prepare any of the no-bake cheesecakes in this book as well.

Serves: 8   **Prep time:** 40 mins

COOKIES AND CRACKERS

MASALA CHEESE WHEAT CRACKERS

'These crackers can add life to any dull party. They're overloaded with a cheesy flavour in every bite; I'm not even exaggerating. The whole wheat flour adds so much flavour too.'

INGREDIENTS

¾ cup (150 g) cheddar cheese
⅓ cup (20 g) Parmesan cheese
¾ cup (100 g) whole wheat flour
60 g or ¼ cup butter, cold
½ tsp salt
¼ tsp garlic powder
1 tsp mixed herbs
½ tsp paprika

STEPS

1. In a mixing bowl, grate in your cheddar cheese, then add the cold chopped butter.
2. Add in the Parmesan cheese, whole wheat flour, salt, garlic powder, mixed herbs and paprika. Then break everything into smaller chunks with the help of a pastry blender or two forks. You could also use a food processor for this task.
3. After everything looks uniform and mixed thoroughly, bring the dough together with your hands. If it feels too dry, add a splash of milk to bind the dough.
4. Then refrigerate the dough for 30 mins and roll it out carefully on a piece of parchment paper. I like to use two silicon mats for rolling, which helps to avoid any sticking.
5. Roll it out to a ½ cm-thick sheet and then prick it with a fork.
6. Using a pizza cutter or a sharp knife, cut small squares or whichever shape you like.
7. Place the dough pieces on a parchment-lined baking sheet while making sure there's enough gap between each piece.
8. Bake in a preheated oven at 180 °C for 10–12 mins or until lightly golden.
9. Let them cool on a wire rack and then store them in an airtight container for up to three weeks.

Pro Tips

1. Use cold ingredients for the recipe and preferably avoid using your hands too much because they can warm up the ingredients, which is not what you want.
2. You can change the flavour combination to make multiple variations. For e.g.: for pizza crackers, you can use oregano and chilli flakes instead of mixed herbs and paprika.

Serves: *14–16*　　　　**Prep time:** *30 mins*　　　　**Bake time:** *12 mins*

MIXED BERRY COOKIES

'These crackers can add life to any dull parties. They're overloaded with a cheesy flavour in every bite, I'm not even exaggerating. The whole wheat flour adds so much flavour too.'

INGREDIENTS

⅓ cup (50 g) fresh or frozen mixed berries
⅓ cup (80 g) unsalted butter, softened
⅓ cup (66 g) caster sugar
½ tsp vanilla extract
1 cup (120 g) all-purpose flour
½ tsp baking powder
A pinch of salt
1 tbsp (15 ml) milk
2 tbsp white chocolate chips
2 tbsp dark chocolate chips
More berries for garnish

STEPS

1. Start by cooking your mixed berries in a saucepan for 2–3 mins or until they look 'jammy'.
2. Then in a bowl, beat the softened butter and sugar for 4–5 mins or until they're creamy.
3. Add in the cooled berries and vanilla extract. Beat for another minute.
4. Then sift in the dry ingredients starting with the all-purpose flour, baking powder and salt.
5. Gently fold until everything is almost combined. Then add in the milk and fold again.
6. Time to add in the chocolate chips. You could also add some extra berries here.
7. Fold again until just combined and refrigerate the dough for 30 mins.
8. Preheat the oven to 190 °C and start scooping the cookie dough onto a parchment-lined baking sheet.
9. Optionally garnish the cookies with chocolate chips and more mixed berries.
10. Bake at 190 °C for 10–12 mins or until the sides are firm but the centre is still soft.
11. Transfer to a wire rack and let them cool for a bit.
12. Enjoy these freshly baked with a cup of coffee.

Pro Tips

1. You can change the flavour of these cookies by altering the fruit used. So instead of mixed berries, you can use just blueberries, or strawberries, or even grapes.
2. Don't over mix the dough and don't overbake the cookies if you want the perfect texture.

Serves: *8–10*   **Prep time:** *30 mins*   **Bake time:** *12 mins*

BROWN BUTTER SKILLET COOKIE

'I wouldn't be lying if I said this is my greatest weakness ever. A freshly baked ooey gooey skillet cookie with a scoop of vanilla ice cream is something I surely cannot resist.'

INGREDIENTS

¼ cup (60 g) butter
¼ cup (50 g) brown sugar
1 large egg yolk
1 tbsp (15 ml) milk
½ tsp vanilla extract
½ cup (120 g) all-purpose flour
¼ tsp baking soda
A pinch of salt
2 tbsp chocolate chunks
2 tbsp chocolate chips

STEPS

1. First things first. Make the brown butter, that's where the flavour comes from.
2. We'll start by cooking our butter on a low heat while mixing occasionally until it turns light brown in colour and smells nutty and aromatic. Then let it cool for 5 mins.
3. Then we'll beat our brown butter and brown sugar for about 3–4 mins.
4. Add in the egg yolk, milk and vanilla extract. Mix it well.
5. Sift in the dry ingredients: the all-purpose flour, baking soda and salt.
6. Cut and fold the dough until it's just combined.
7. Add in the dark chocolate chunks and chocolate chips.
8. Combine everything and refrigerate the dough for 30 mins.
9. Preheat your oven to 180 °C.
10. Take a 6–7-inch skillet and spread the cookie dough in it.
11. Top it off with extra chocolate chips and bake in a preheated oven at 180 °C for 14–15 mins.
12. Let it cool for just 2–4 mins and top it off with a scoop of vanilla ice cream and chocolate syrup.
    Indulge in the best cookie you have ever tasted. This is just perfect for a party.

Pro Tips

1. Measure the brown butter after you cool it because there will be some moisture loss during the procedure which may alter the ratios. You can also add some water if you're falling short of butter.
2. You can substitute the egg yolk with 2 tbsp milk to make this recipe eggless.
3. Use really good-quality chocolate chips for the best results.

Serves: *6–7* **Prep time:** *30 mins* **Bake time:** *15 mins*

KASHMIRI LAAL MIRCH COOKIES

'When I saw a viral recipe from Korea called Gochujang Caramel Cookies, I thought why not infuse our Indian chillies in cookies, which resulted in the most unique sweet chilli combo.'

INGREDIENTS

½ cup (120 g) unsalted butter, softened
1 cup (200 g) caster sugar
1 tsp vanilla extract
3 tbsp (45 ml) milk
1 ½ cup (180 g) all-purpose flour
¾ tsp salt
½ tsp baking soda
¼ tsp cinnamon powder
2 tbsp (25 g) light brown sugar
1 tbsp Kashmiri laal mirch paste
1 tbsp butter, softened

STEPS

1. Firstly, immerse some Kashmiri laal chillies in some boiling hot water for 7–8 mins. Then de-seed and blend them to get a smooth paste.
2. Then start creaming the butter and sugar together for 5–6 mins.
3. Add in the vanilla extract and milk. Combine everything well.
4. Sift in the all-purpose flour, baking soda, cinnamon and salt.
5. Gently fold to form a dough. Then keep it aside.
6. In a separate bowl, combine the Kashmiri chilli paste, brown sugar and softened butter.
7. Then dollop this mixture unevenly in your dough and gently fold so that there are streaks of Kashmiri chilli in the dough.
8. Refrigerate the dough for 30 mins.
9. Then preheat the oven to 170 °C.
10. Shape and bake the cookies in a parchment-lined baking sheet at 170 °C for 15–17 mins or until set around the edges.
11. Let them cool on a wire rack and enjoy them while fresh.

Pro Tips
1. You can make this recipe with eggs, by just replacing the milk with a whole egg.
2. Feel free to use a Gochujang chilli paste (Korean chilli paste) instead of Kashmiri laal mirch paste to make the original version of the recipe.

Serves: *8–9*　　　**Prep time:** *35 mins*　　　**Bake time:** *17 mins*

SWISS MERINGUE MOCHA MACARONS

'This is the dish that got me obsessed with baking and led to my baking spree. I failed at baking macarons seven to eight times before baking my first successful batch. I was obsessed with them afterwards. I have baked thousands of macarons so far, but this flavour hits the spot.'

INGREDIENTS

For the Ganache
200 g dark chocolate
100 g cream
2 tsp instant coffee powder

For the Macarons
52 g almond flour
52 g icing sugar
50 g egg whites
50 g caster sugar
1 tsp instant coffee powder

STEPS

1. Heat the fresh cream or whipping cream in a double boiler set-up or a microwave until it starts to bubble, then add in the instant coffee powder and mix.
2. Add your chopped dark chocolate to the cream. Mix everything and let the chocolate melt. Then remove the bowl from double boiler and let it chill for 3–4 hours.
3. Take a super-clean bowl, wipe it down with vinegar to ensure there's no grease or fat stuck on it. Add in the egg whites and caster sugar in it. Place it on a double boiler set-up and heat on low for a couple of minutes until all of the sugar is completely dissolved. This will take only 1–2 mins. Remove from heat.
4. Start beating at a low speed and continue increasing the speed of the beater while whipping. When soft peaks are achieved, continue whipping for another minute until stiff peaks form.
5. Sift all the dry ingredients and add to the wet ingredients. Start folding using the cut and fold method; don't over mix. Fold until you reach a lava-like consistency; the batter shouldn't be too flowy, but it should slowly fall off the spatula. You can also perform a figure 8 test by dropping some batter back in the bowl in an 'infinity' or '8' motion. The batter should form multiple figure 8s before breaking.
6. Then pipe your macarons using a piping bag with a round nozzle. Dust some instant coffee on them.
7. Let them rest for 30–60 mins until a skin is formed on top. If possible, keep them in an air-conditioned space.
8. Then bake in a preheated oven at 150 °C for 20 mins (turning every 5–10 mins).
9. Keep them at room temperature and then fill with the ganache. Store them in the fridge in an airtight container for at least 24 hours before you indulge in them. This allows them to develop a unique chewy texture.

Serves: *18–20*   **Prep time:** *40 mins*   **Bake time:** *20 mins*

ULTRA-FUDGY BROOKIES

'This cross between chewy chocolate chip cookies and fudgy brownies is surely one of the best things you will ever taste. They're ooey gooey, fudgy and super rich in flavour.'

INGREDIENTS

½ cup (120 g) unsalted butter, melted

½ cup (50 g) cocoa powder

1 tsp coffee

½ cup (100 g) caster sugar

½ cup (100 g) brown sugar

1 large egg

1 tsp vanilla essence

⅔ cup (80 g) all-purpose flour

½ tsp salt

½ tsp baking powder

⅓ cup dark chocolate chips

2 tbsp hot water

STEPS

1. Start by combining the melted butter with cocoa powder and instant coffee.
2. In a separate bowl, beat the egg with caster sugar and brown sugar for 5 mins.
3. Then add in the butter mixture and vanilla extract. Combine everything well.
4. Sift in the all-purpose flour, salt and baking powder. Fold to combine everything.
5. Time to add in some hot water and mix it in.
6. Lastly, add in some good-quality dark chocolate chips and mix one last time.
7. Refrigerate the dough for 30 mins.
8. Preheat your oven to 170 °C and scoop the cookie dough onto a parchment-lined baking sheet.
9. Then bake in a preheated oven at 170 °C for 12–13 mins.
10. Let them cool on a wire rack for a few minutes and enjoy them warm.

Pro Tips

1. Always use good-quality dark chocolate chips or callets to get the best results.
2. Chilling the dough will help to firm it so that it's easier to scoop. But it also helps with gluten relaxation.
3. If you're using salted butter for any of the recipes, then skip adding extra salt.

Serves: *7–8*   **Prep time:** *25 mins*   **Bake time:** *13 mins*

ALMOND CRANBERRY ORANGE BISCOTTI

'This flavour combination is truly just wow and these biscottis pair wonderfully well with some tea or coffee.'

INGREDIENTS

2 eggs
¼ cup (60 ml) oil
¾ cup (150 g) sugar
1 tsp vanilla extract
A few drops almond extract (optional)
1 tsp orange zest
1 ¾ cup (210 g) all-purpose flour
¼ tsp salt
1 tsp baking powder
½ cup (50 g) dried cranberries
1 cup (130 g) almonds

STEPS

1. In a mixing bowl, beat the eggs and sugar for a minute using a whisk.
2. Then add in the oil, vanilla extract, almond extract and orange zest. Combine well.
3. Sift in the all-purpose flour, salt and baking powder. Mix everything evenly.
4. Then add in the almonds and cranberries, mix well.
5. Transfer the dough into a wide lined loaf tin (around 9 inches by 4.5 inches).
6. Bake in a preheated oven at 160 °C for 30 mins. Let it cool completely.
7. Then cut into biscottis, place them on a parchment-lined baking sheet and bake again at 140 °C for 10 mins.
8. Serve with tea or coffee.

Pro Tips

1. You can use 2 flax eggs in place of eggs to make this recipe vegan (refer to the egg substitution section of this book on page ix).
2. Feel free to change the flavour combination by altering the nuts and fruits used.
3. Instead of using a loaf tin you can also just shape the dough into a thick sheet and bake directly on a baking sheet. This results in more rugged, rusty-looking biscottis.

Serves: 20–25   **Prep time:** 30 mins   **Bake time:** 40 mins

TARTS AND PIES

BRÛLÉED WALNUT BANOFFEE PIE

'While I was writing this book, I went on a walnut harvest tour in California. While I was there, I was constantly thinking of unique, lip-smacking desserts and I came up with this one.'

INGREDIENTS

For the Crust

160 g biscuits
⅓ cup (80 g) butter, melted

For the Dulce De Leche

1 can (400 g or 1 ¾ cup) sweetened condensed milk

For the Filling

4–5 bananas, sliced lengthwise
1 cup (120 g) walnuts, roasted

For the Topping

¼ cup (50 g) caster sugar
Some dark chocolate shavings

STEPS

1. Place the condensed milk can in a pressure cooker and fill the cooker with water. The can should be completely submerged and the water should a few inches above the can.
2. Then close the lid and let it cook at medium flame until the first whistle goes off.
3. Lower the flame and let it cook for 15–17 mins more. Turn off the flame and let the cooker de pressurize naturally. This will take at least an hour.
4. Let the can come down to room temperature as well.
5. Open the can carefully and you have just made yourself an easy and delicious dulce de leche.
6. For the crust, crush your biscuits until they are slightly coarse in texture. Make sure there are no big chunks. Add in your melted butter and stir to combine.
7. Transfer the mixture to a greased pie tin or dish. Spread it evenly and press it down firmly. Refrigerate this for 15 mins. Slice your bananas lengthwise and keep them aside. Remove your prepared crust from the fridge and top it off with that creamy dulce de leche. Spread it evenly. Then add a layer of roasted walnuts.
8. Top it off with sliced bananas. Make sure to arrange them evenly. Refrigerate overnight.
9. Top this all up with some caster sugar and brûlée it using a blow torch.
10. Garnish with some chocolate shavings and enjoy.

Pro Tip

1. *Generally, whipped cream is added on top, but since in this version we are brûlée-ing it, I have skipped that. You can however still add that in place of the brûlée element.*

Serves: *8*   **Prep time:** *60 mins*

MONOGRAM CHOCOLATE TART CAKE

'So, the "P" in the image stands for "Plated by Parth" and not "Parth", just to clarify ;) This is probably the most customizable recipe ever. Perfect for celebrations of all kinds.'

INGREDIENTS

For the Short Crust Pastry
1 cup (120 g) all-purpose flour
½ cup (50 g) icing sugar
½ cup (113 g) unsalted butter, cold and chopped

For the Chocolate Ganache
1⅓ cup (200 g) dark chocolate
¾ cup + 1 tbsp (100 g) cream

STEPS

1. Mix together the flour and the sugar really well. Then add in cold chopped unsalted butter.
2. Start breaking the butter in the flour using hands or a whisk or a pastry cutter. You can use a food processor too. The texture should look like breadcrumbs, then form a dough by pressing it. If it is too hard after mixing for 1–2 mins, add 1–2 tbsp of cold water.
3. Form a dough and plastic wrap it. Refrigerate it for 1 hour.
4. Then roll onto a parchment paper or silicon mat while it's cold and cut into the desired shape.
5. Bake it in a 170 °C preheated oven for 8–12 mins.
6. It should be done when you see the edges getting a light golden-brown colour. You can bake 2–3 layers per design to stack them up.
7. For the ganache, heat the fresh cream in a double boiler set-up or microwave.
8. Put in the chopped chocolate, and let it sit for 1–2 mins.
9. Then, mix till a smooth mixture is formed. Let it cool completely before keeping it in the fridge for 1–2 hours until set and then add to a piping bag.
10. Pipe dollops of chocolate ganache on the first layer and then top it off with the second layer or the tart. Finish with another layer of the ganache and add your favourite toppings like fruits, nuts, chocolates, wafers and flowers.

Pro Tips

1. *For cutting the desired shapes, you can print stencils of various letters or numbers, as per your desired size and then place your parchment paper above it to trace them. Then, simply cut the dough using those custom stencils as a guide.*

2. *You can freeze the tart dough and bake custom tart cakes with it whenever you need to.*

3. *You can make white chocolate ganache by taking 300 g white chocolate instead of 200 g dark chocolate.*

Serves: *7–8*   **Prep time:** *45 mins*   **Bake time:** *12 mins*

TRADITIONAL APPLE PIE

'Apple was the first pie I ever baked, and it just stuck. It always feels nostalgic to bake it, and when served with vanilla ice cream, it becomes irresistible.'

INGREDIENTS

For the Pie Dough

2 ½ cup (315 g) all-purpose flour
1 tsp salt
¾ cup (168 g) unsalted butter, cold and cubed
6–8 tbsp cold water as needed

For the Filling

750 g peeled apples
2 tbsp all-purpose flour
¾ cup brown sugar
½ tsp cinnamon
¼ tsp nutmeg
1 tsp lemon juice

STEPS

1. For the pie dough, start by mixing the flour and salt. Then add in the cold, chopped butter. Then blend it together using a pastry blender/whisk/two forks. You can even use a food processor for this.
2. After a few minutes, the butter and flour mixture will look like breadcrumbs, at which point we will start adding our cold water in this, 1 tbsp at a time. Combine to form a tight dough. Refrigerate the dough for a couple of hours.
3. For the filling, peel and chop the apples into small or medium pieces. Then add in the brown sugar, all-purpose flour, cinnamon, nutmeg and lemon juice in this.
4. Then combine everything really well.
5. Roll out half of the pie dough on a silicon mat or parchment paper. Then place it nicely in a greased 10-inch pie tin. Press firmly on the sides to shape the crust. Trim off the excess dough using a knife and then prick the entire dough using a fork.
6. Put in as much filling as the pie can hold and then roll the second half of the dough and top it off on the pie in any creative way that you like. I went with a lattice-style design.
7. Optionally egg wash and top it off with some caster sugar. Then bake in a preheated oven at 200 °C for 50–55 mins or golden on top. Let it cool down to room temperature.
8. Then cut and top it off with a scoop of vanilla ice cream.

Pro Tip

1. *You can follow the egg substitution for the egg wash, which is mentioned in the egg substitutions section of this book, on page ix.*

Serves: *8*   **Prep time:** *50 mins*   **Bake time:** *55 mins*

BLUEBERRY CRUMBLE

'This one is my friend's favourite party dessert that I bake for them. It *always* gets over within seconds, not even kidding. Especially when it's served warm with ice cream.'

INGREDIENTS

For the Dough

1 cup (120 g) all-purpose flour
¼ tsp baking powder
⅓ cup (66 g) caster sugar
A pinch of salt
⅓ cup (80 g) butter, cold
1 tsp vanilla
1 tbsp milk or 1 egg yolk
1 tsp vinegar

For the Filling

1 ½ cup of blueberries
Zest of a small lemon
1 tsp lemon juice
2 tbsp caster sugar
2 tsp cornflour

STEPS

1. For the pie dough, start by mixing the flour, baking powder, caster sugar and salt. Then add in the cold chopped butter. Then blend it together using a food processor or a pastry blender. You can even use two forks or whisk for this.
2. Once you reach a breadcrumb-like consistency, add in the vanilla extract, milk and vinegar. Combine everything together to form a dough.
3. Preheat your oven to 180 °C. Meanwhile, prepare the filling by combining blueberries, lemon zest, lemon juice, caster sugar and cornflour.
4. Grease your skillet with butter and add two-third of the dough in it. Press it down to form the crust and top it off with all of your blueberry filling.
5. Randomly add the remaining dough on top of the berry filling.
6. Bake in a preheated oven at 180 °C for 40–45 mins.
7. Let it cool down for 10 mins and top it off with some vanilla ice cream.
8. Dig in the most epic dessert ever.

Pro Tips

1. You can make a strawberry crumble, raspberry crumble or a mixed berry crumble with this same recipe.
2. You don't even need to use egg yolk in this recipe, the milk works out just fine.

Serves: *6–7*　　　**Prep time:** *35 mins*　　　**Bake time:** *45 mins*

NO-BAKE LEMON MERINGUE PIE

'This was the first dish I ever shot while writing this book, so it only seems fair to end it with this one. I feel like the book has come full circle.'

INGREDIENTS

For the Crust
160 g biscuits
⅓ cup (80 g) butter, melted

For the Filling
¼ cup (60 ml) lemon juice
1 tsp lemon zest
⅓ cup (66 g) sugar
A pinch of salt
1 tbsp (15 ml) water
1 tbsp cornflour
¼ cup (60 g) unsalted butter
¼ cup (80 g) condensed milk

For the Meringue
¼ cup (60 ml) of aquafaba (chickpea water). You can use egg whites too
66 g caster sugar or ⅓ cup caster sugar
¼ tsp lemon juice
A pinch of cream of tartar

STEPS

1. For the crust, crush your biscuits until they are slightly coarse in texture. Make sure there are no big chunks. Add in your melted butter and stir to combine.
2. Transfer the mixture to a greased pie tin or dish. Spread it evenly and press it down firmly. Refrigerate for 15 mins.
3. Meanwhile, in a saucepan, add lemon juice, lemon zest, sugar and salt. Stir everything and cook until it starts boiling.
4. Then add in a slurry of water and cornflour. After that stir constantly until the mixture thickens a bit. This should take around 2–3 mins, then add in your butter.
5. Let the butter melt completely and emulsify in the curd. Then turn off the flame.
6. Add in your condensed milk and refrigerate. Your lemon curd is ready.
7. Pour this in your prepared crust and spread evenly. Skin wrap it using cling wrap and refrigerate for 6 hours or overnight.
8. Whip up the aquafaba with cream of tartar and lemon juice at a high speed for 2 mins until it's thick and foamy. Then turn the speed to low and add the sugar in batches and continue to beat for 5–6 mins or until stiff peaks form. Spread the meringue on top of the lemon curd layer and torch it up using a blow torch. Serve fresh.

Serves: 8　　　　**Prep time:** 50–55 mins

Acknowledgements

I would like to express my deepest gratitude to everyone who made this baking cookbook possible. This journey has been an exciting and rewarding experience, and it wouldn't have been the same without the support and contributions of so many.

First and foremost, I want to thank my family and friends for their unwavering encouragement. Especially for always being there when I needed a taste tester or a helping hand in the kitchen. A big thank you to my sister-in-law, Khushi Bajaj, for helping me with this!

A special thanks to my team—Simran Nashine and Devendra Kumbhare—for their invaluable support and expertise throughout the creation of this book. Your ideas and efforts made a world of difference.

I'd also like to thank team Penguin India, especially Gurveen and Manali, for believing in this project and helping bring it to life. Your insight and guidance made all the difference in shaping the vision of this cookbook.

Special thanks to the team who helped me shoot the cover for the book. Major thanks and gratitude to my dear friend Khushboo Soni for shooting the cover along with her team. My best friends, Omkar Bhatia and Tanay Shahu, for assisting us during the shoot.

To my readers and fellow food enthusiasts, I hope this book brings as much joy and satisfaction to your kitchen as it has brought to mine.

Lastly, I dedicate this book to all the budding bakers out there; your passion for food continues to inspire me every day.

Thank you to each and every one who has played a part in this journey. Your support has been a gift, and I am forever grateful.

Scan QR code to access the
Penguin Random House India website